"With uncommon clarity and kindness, the author speaks directly to the invisible heart of childhood abuse—shame. Readers will recognize the authentic voice of a former victim as she gently guides them on the healing path to self-compassion. It is an artful distillation of self-compassion theory, research, and practice for those who have suffered long enough. I can't recommend it highly enough."

—**Christopher Germer, PhD,** clinical instructor at Harvard Medical School and author of *The Mindful Path to Self-Compassion*

"This book provides an in-depth understanding of the many ways shame sustains the harm of past abuse, and outlines a powerful program for using self-compassion to free yourself from these bonds. Read it and heal."

—**Kristin Neff, PhD,** author of *Self-Compassion*

"In this beautifully written book, Beverley Engel offers us a scholarly, yet easily-accessible understanding of the nature of shame and the harm that it does us. She also articulates very clearly how compassion is one of the most important antidotes for shame. After all, it's easy to be compassionate toward people we like—but real compassion is for when things get tough. No one can read this book without coming away with considerable insights into the problematic ways we often treat ourselves and the value of developing compassion—not just as an easy option, but as a courageous way to deal with our inner struggles. I can't recommend this book highly enough; it is well-researched, highly informative, and helpful. A real gift to those struggling with the inner conflicts of self-doubt and criticism."

—**Paul Gilbert, PhD,** author of *The Compassionate Mind*

"What a wonderful book! Beverly Engel has a deep understanding of how abuse and neglect affect children. Once again, she has written a much-needed, breakthrough book for those recovering from abuse. This time, she presents a profoundly powerful program to help survivors overcome one of the most devastating effects of abuse—debilitating shame. In it she teaches survivors how to practice self-compassion—an amazing healing tool. I highly recommend this book to anyone who was abused or neglected in childhood or adulthood."

—**Susan Forward, PhD,** author of *Toxic Parents* and *Mothers Who Can't Love*

It Wasn't Your Fault

*Freeing Yourself from the
Shame of Childhood Abuse with
the Power of Self-Compassion*

Beverly Engel, LMFT

New Harbinger Publications, Inc.

Publisher's Note

This publication is designed to provide accurate and authoritative information in regard to the subject matter covered. It is sold with the understanding that the publisher is not engaged in rendering psychological, financial, legal, or other professional services. If expert assistance or counseling is needed, the services of a competent professional should be sought.

Distributed in Canada by Raincoast Books

Copyright © 2015 by Beverly Engel
New Harbinger Publications, Inc.
5674 Shattuck Avenue
Oakland, CA 94609
http://www.newharbinger.com

Cover design by Amy Shoup
Acquired by Melissa Kirk
Edited by Clancy Drake

Library of Congress Cataloging-in-Publication Data

Engel, Beverly.
  It wasn't your fault : freeing yourself from the shame of childhood abuse with the power of self-compassion / Beverly Engel.
    pages cm
  Includes bibliographical references.
  ISBN 978-1-62625-099-4 (paperback) -- ISBN 978-1-62625-100-7 (pdf e-book) -- ISBN 978-1-62625-101-4 (epub) 1. Adult child abuse victims. 2. Shame. 3. Self-esteem. I. Title.
  RC569.5.C55E54 2015
  616.85'822390651--dc23

                        2014039183

Printed in the United States of America

22   21   20

15   14   13   12   11   10   9   8

I dedicate this book to all my clients, past and present, who inspire me, inform me, and heal me. Your strength, courage, and determination are awe-inspiring.

Contents

Part III
Practicing the Five Aspects of Self-Compassion

Acknowledgments

I am deeply grateful for the wise teachers, researchers, and authors who helped me to understand shame, compassion, and self-compassion on a much deeper level. First and foremost I wish to thank Gershen Kaufman for his brilliant work on shame, including his book *Shame: The Power of Caring*. No one understands the subject of shame quite as much as you seem to and I am so grateful I found your work. Next, I would like to thank those in the Restorative Justice movement who taught me that it is not through shaming that we rehabilitate offenders, but through compassion.

I am deeply indebted to Kristin Neff for her outstanding research on self-compassion, her excellent book *Self-Compassion,* and her website, http://www.selfcompassion.org, which not only helped me in the writing of this book but have helped many of my clients tremendously. I especially wish to thank Paul Gilbert, author of *The Compassionate Mind* and one of the leading researchers on self-compassion as a therapeutic tool, for his extensive research on compassion, especially as it relates to shame.

I also wish to thank Christopher Germer for his excellent book *The Mindful Path to Self-Compassion*, and Tara Brach for her revolutionary book *Radical Acceptance*, both excellent resources for myself and my clients. Last, but certainly not least, I wish to acknowledge the Dalai Lama, Mahatma Gandhi, Nelson Mandela, and Martin Luther King, Jr., all great men who taught us that it is through compassion that we will heal the world.

A special thank you to everyone at New Harbinger, and especially to freelance copy editor Clancy Drake, whose fine editing helped make the book the best it could be.

Introduction

Mine has been a life of much shame. I can't even guess
what it must be to live the life of a human being.

—Osamu Dazai

If you were a victim of childhood abuse or neglect you know about
shame. You have likely been plagued by it all your life. You may feel
shame because you blame yourself for the abuse itself ("My father
wouldn't have hit me if I had minded him"), or because you felt such
humiliation at having been abused ("I feel like such a wimp for not
defending myself"). While those who were sexually abused tend to
suffer from the most shame, those who suffered from physical, verbal,
or emotional abuse blame themselves as well. In the case of child
sexual abuse, no matter how many times you have heard the words
"It's not your fault," the chances are high that you still blame yourself
in some way—for being submissive, for not telling someone and
having the abuse continue, for "enticing" the abuser with your
behavior or dress, or because you felt some physical pleasure.

In the case of physical, verbal, and emotional abuse, you may
blame yourself for "not listening" and thus making your parent or
other caretaker so angry that he or she yelled at you or hit you.
Children tend to blame the neglect and abuse they experience on
themselves, in essence saying to themselves, "My mother is treating
me like this because I've been bad," or, "I am being neglected because
I am unlovable." As an adult you may have continued this kind of
rationalization, putting up with poor treatment by others because
you believe you brought it on yourself. Conversely, when good things

happen to you, you may actually become uncomfortable, because you feel so unworthy.

You may also have a great deal of shame due to the exposure of the abuse. If you reported the abuse to someone, you may blame yourself for the consequences of your outcry—your parents divorcing, your molester going to jail, your family going to court.

And there is the shame you may feel about your behavior that was a consequence of the abuse. Former victims of childhood abuse tend to feel a great deal of shame for things they did as children as a result of the abuse. For example, perhaps unable to express their anger at an abuser, they may have taken their hurt and anger out on those who were smaller or weaker than themselves, such as younger siblings. They may have become bullies at school, been belligerent toward authority figures, or started stealing, taking drugs, or otherwise acting out against society. In the case of sexual abuse, former victims may have continued the cycle of abuse by introducing younger children to sex.

You may also feel shame because of things you have done as an adult to hurt yourself and others, such as abusing alcohol or drugs, becoming sexually promiscuous, or breaking the law. Adults who were abused as children may push away those who try to be good to them; become emotionally or physically abusive to their partners; or continue a pattern of being abused, subjecting their own children to witnessing abuse or, worse, being abused themselves. Former abuse victims may repeat the cycle of abuse by emotionally, physically, or sexually abusing their own children, or may abandon their children because they can't take care of them.

It's Not Your Fault will explore such manifestations of shame in a way that will help you understand yourself and your behavior better. Such understanding can allow you to forgive yourself and, finally, to rid yourself of the shame that may have crippled you in many ways. The truth is that for most victims of abuse, shame is likely one of the worst effects of the abuse or neglect, possibly the very worst. Unless they are able to heal this debilitating shame, they will likely continue to suffer many problems in life.

How Shame Affects Victims of Abuse

If you were a victim of childhood abuse or neglect, shame can affect literally every aspect of your life: from your self-confidence, self-esteem, and body image to your ability to relate to others, navigate intimate relationships, and be a good parent; from your work performance to your ability to learn new things or care for yourself. Shame is responsible for myriad personal problems, including:

- Self-criticism and self-blame

- Self-neglect

- Self-destructive behaviors (such as abusing your body with too much or too little food, alcohol, drugs, or cigarettes, self-mutilation, or being accident-prone)

- Self-sabotaging behavior (such as starting fights with loved ones or sabotaging jobs)

- Perfectionism (based on fear of being caught in a mistake)

- Believing you don't deserve good things

- Believing if others really knew you they would dislike or be disgusted by you

- People-pleasing

- Tending to be critical of others (trying to give shame away)

- Intense rage (frequent physical fights or road rage)

- Acting out against society (breaking rules or laws)

- Repeating the cycle of abuse through victim behavior and/or abusive behavior

Victims of child abuse are typically changed by the experience, not only because they were traumatized, but because they feel a loss of innocence and dignity and they carry forward a heavy burden of shame. Emotional, physical, and sexual child abuse can so overwhelm a victim with shame that it actually comes to define the person, keeping her from her full potential. It can cause a victim both to remain fixed at the age he was at the time of his victimization and to repeat the abuse over and over in his lifetime.

Shame is at the core of every form of abuse; it deeply informs the behavior of both abusers and victims. Shame drives the cycle of abuse in several ways:

⚘ Shame can keep former victims from believing they deserve to be treated with love, kindness, and respect; one result is that they may stay in abusive relationships.

⚘ Shame can cause former victims to believe they deserve to be treated with disrespect and disdain.

⚘ Shame can cause a person to humiliate and degrade his partner or children.

⚘ Those who abuse others are often trying to rid themselves of their own shame.

⚘ Shame can cause emotional outbursts, fueling the rage that triggers abusiveness.

Shame from childhood abuse almost always manifests itself in one or more of these ways:

⚘ It causes abuse victims to abuse themselves with critical self-talk, alcohol or drug abuse, destructive eating patterns, and/or other forms of self-harm. Two-thirds of people in treatment for drug abuse reported being abused or neglected as children (Swan 1998).

⚘ It causes abuse victims to develop victim-like behavior, whereby they expect and accept unacceptable, abusive behavior from others. As many as 90 percent of women in battered women's shelters report having been abused or neglected as children (U.S. Department of Health and Human Services 2013).

❀ It causes abuse victims to become abusive. About 30 percent of abused and neglected children will later abuse their own children (U.S. Department of Health and Human Services 2013).

Facing the problems that shame has created in your life can be daunting. You may be overwhelmed with the problem of how to heal the shame caused by the childhood abuse you experienced. The good news is that you are not alone; there are thousands upon thousands of former victims who are facing the same problems. The even better news is that there is a way to heal your shame. *It's Not Your Fault* will take you on a step-by-step journey to heal your shame and begin to see the world through different eyes—eyes not clouded by the perception that you are "less than," inadequate, damaged, worthless, or unlovable.

The Healing Power of Compassion and Self-Compassion

Several years ago, I became conscious of a source of increasing frustration in my work. I had been a psychotherapist specializing in working with victims of childhood abuse for thirty-five years, yet I continued to struggle to find effective ways to help my clients eliminate the debilitating shame from which they suffered. I wasn't alone: many psychotherapists and advocates working with adult survivors of child abuse have long understood that shame is among the most enduring effects of abuse, and that our clients have an especially difficult time working through it. And I had my own experience of shame's persistence: after many years of therapy, I still struggled with my own shame due to my abuse experiences as a child.

I resolved to find a way to help victims of childhood abuse recover from shame, which I increasingly considered the worst aftereffect of their trauma. After over five years of study and research, I concluded that *compassion* is the remedy for shame. Like a poison, toxic shame needs to be neutralized by another substance—an antidote—if the patient is to be saved. Compassion is the only thing that can counteract the isolating, stigmatizing, debilitating poison of shame.

I was well aware of how healing compassion could be for my clients. I knew well the work of Alice Miller, who believed that what victims of childhood abuse need most is what she called a "compassionate witness" to validate their experiences and support them through their pain (Miller 1984). I had personally experienced how my being a compassionate witness was healing for my clients, as well as how transformative my having a compassionate therapist had been for me.

In recent years, many researchers have taken up the subject of compassion. Their work has revealed, among other insights, that the kindness, support, encouragement, and compassion of others have a huge impact on how our brains, bodies, and general sense of well-being develop. Love and kindness, especially in early life, even affect how some of our genes are expressed (Gilbert 2009, Cozolino 2007).

As I continued my research, I discovered that while I had come to understand more fully the healing powers of compassion, I hadn't truly recognized the importance of *self-compassion*—extending compassion to oneself in instances of perceived inadequacy, failure, or general suffering—in the treatment of psychotherapy clients, particularly former victims of child abuse. In 2003, Kristin Neff published the first two articles defining and measuring self-compassion (Neff 2003a, Neff 2003b); before this, the subject of self-compassion had never been formally studied. There have since been over two hundred journal articles and dissertations on self-compassion.

One of the most consistent findings in this research literature is that greater self-compassion is linked to less psychopathology (Barnard and Curry 2011). And a recent meta-analysis showed self-compassion to have a positive effect on depression, anxiety, and stress across twenty studies (MacBeth and Gumley 2012).

Self-compassion also appears to facilitate resilience by moderating people's reactions to negative events—trauma in particular. Gilbert and Procter (2006) suggest that self-compassion provides emotional resilience because it deactivates the threat system. And it has been found that abused individuals with higher levels of self-compassion are better able to cope with upsetting events (Vettese et al. 2011).

There is evidence that self-compassion helps people diagnosed with post-traumatic stress disorder (PTSD). In one study of college students who showed PTSD symptoms after experiencing a traumatic event such as an accident or life-threatening illness, those with more self-compassion showed less severe symptoms than those who lacked self-compassion. In particular, they were less likely to display signs of emotional avoidance and more comfortable facing the thoughts, feelings, and sensations associated with the trauma they experienced (Thompson and Waltz 2008).

Finally, in addition to self-compassion being a key factor in helping those who were traumatized in childhood, it turns out that self-compassion is the missing key to alleviating shame. Confirming what I knew from my extensive work with former victims of child abuse, research shows that traumatized individuals feel significant levels of shame and/or guilt (Jonsson and Segesten 2004). Shame has been recognized as a major component of a range of mental health problems as well as proneness to aggression (Gilbert 1997, Gilbert 2003, Gilligan 2003, Tangney and Dearing 2002). And it has been found that decreases in anxiety, shame, and guilt and increases in the willingness to express sadness, anger, and closeness were associated with higher levels of self-compassion (Germer and Neff 2013).

I even found a clinician who was utilizing self-compassion to help people who suffer from severe shame and self-judgment: Paul Gilbert, author of *The Compassionate Mind*. A study of the effectiveness of Gilbert's Compassionate Mind Training (CMT)—a group-based therapy model that works specifically with shame, guilt, and self-blame—found that the training resulted in significant reductions in depression, self-attacking, feelings of inferiority, and shame (Gilbert and Procter 2006).

In addition, research suggests that self-compassion can act as an antidote to self-criticism—a major characteristic of those who experience intense shame (Gilbert and Miles 2000). Self-compassion is a powerful trigger for the release of oxytocin, the hormone that increases feelings of trust, calm, safety, generosity, and connectedness. Self-criticism has a very different effect on our bodies. The amygdala, the oldest part of the brain, is designed to quickly detect threats in the environment. These trigger the fight-or-flight response—the amygdala sends signals that increase blood pressure, adrenaline, and cortisol, mobilizing the strength and energy needed to confront or avoid the threat. Although this system was designed by evolution to deal with physical attacks, it is activated just as readily by emotional attacks—from ourselves and others. Over time, increased cortisol levels deplete neurotransmitters involved in the ability to experience pleasure, leading to depression (Gilbert 2005).

Neurological evidence also shows that self-kindness (a major component of self-compassion) and self-criticism operate quite differently in terms of brain function. A recent study examined reactions to personal failure using fMRI (functional magnetic resonance imaging) technology. While in a brain scanner, participants were presented with hypothetical situations such as "A third job rejection letter in a row arrives in the mail." They were then told to imagine reacting to the situation in either a kind or a self-critical way. Self-criticism was associated with activity in the lateral prefrontal cortex and dorsal anterior cingulate—areas of the brain associated with error processing and problem solving. Being kind and reassuring toward oneself was associated with left temporal pole and insula activation—areas of the brain associated with positive emotions and compassion (Longe et al. 2010). As Kristin Neff (2011) aptly stated, "Instead of seeing ourselves as a problem to be fixed…self-kindness allows us to see ourselves as valuable human beings who are worthy of care."

Of particular interest to me was recent research in the neurobiology of compassion as it relates to shame—namely that we now know some of the neurobiological correlates of feeling unlovable and how shame gets stuck in our neural circuitry. Moreover, and most crucially of all, due to our brains' capacity to grow new neurons and new synaptic connections, we can proactively repair (and re-pair) old shame memories with new experiences of self-empathy and self-compassion.

In light of my research, I determined that in addition to offering my clients compassion for their suffering, I needed to teach them how to practice self-compassion on an ongoing basis in order to heal the many layers of shame they experience.

Self-compassion as a healing tool is a relatively new concept. For many years therapists have taught their clients how to nurture their "inner child," a successful therapeutic strategy in many ways. But teaching self-compassion goes further. It helps victims connect with their childhood suffering much more deeply. It allows them to connect with the memories of their abuse, but at a distance—not actually reexperiencing the abuse but remembering it as if they have become their own compassionate witness. They can thus develop compassion for the child they once were without *becoming* the child. This method both reduces the chance the person will be re-traumatized by the memories and allows her to become the loving guardian and protector she so longed for as a child. It provides her a way to heal herself, and to learn to treat herself *today* in a more loving and kind way.

The Compassion Cure Program

Combining what I learned about compassion and self-compassion with the wisdom I've gleaned from my many years of working with victims of childhood abuse, I created a program specifically aimed at helping those who experienced abuse become free of debilitating shame. My Compassion Cure program combines groundbreaking scientific research on self-compassion, compassion, shame, and restorative justice with real-life case examples (modified to protect the subjects' anonymity). Its proprietary processes and exercises help abuse victims reduce or eliminate the shame that has weighed them down and kept them stuck in the past.

By learning to practice self-compassion, you will rid yourself of shame-based beliefs, such as that you are worthless, defective, bad, or unlovable. Abuse victims often cope with these false yet powerful beliefs by trying to ignore them or convince themselves otherwise by puffing themselves up, overachieving, or becoming perfectionistic. These strategies take huge amounts of energy, and they are not effective. Rather, actively approaching, recognizing, validating, and understanding shame is the way to overcome it.

Instead of denying your shame and the feelings it engenders, bring it out into the light. Instead of feeling shame about your shame, work toward acceptance of it. Instead of constantly seeking approval and recognition from outside yourself, learn to value yourself from within. My Compassion Cure program, based on the practice of self-compassion, will help you accomplish these tasks.

My Story: Joyfulness Extinguished by Abuse, Neglect, and Shame

Although I created my Compassion Cure program to help my clients who suffered from debilitating shame, my interest in the subject of shame and how to heal it originated in my own struggles with it. Ridding myself of the shame I experienced as a result of the neglect and the emotional, sexual, and physical abuse I suffered as a child has been the most difficult endeavor of my life. Shame defined who I was as a child and who I became as an adult. It influenced how I felt about myself, took care of myself, perceived my body and my sexuality, and interacted with others; who I chose as friends and romantic partners; and even my career choice.

Because I suffered from all three major types of abuse, as well as neglect, I feel I can personally identify with any abuse victim reading this book. While there are no doubt many differences in our stories, I can assure you there are many similarities as well. Those of us who experienced abuse and neglect in childhood are a unique tribe, and we can gain much from supporting one another. I hope this book will serve as my way to connect with you and offer you the wisdom I gleaned both from healing from my own abuse and from working with clients for so long. I'll also share with you some of my personal experience of shame, as well as my journey toward healing.

Although I can't remember a time when I didn't feel shame, I have evidence that there was such a time. I have a photograph of me at about six months old, smiling, with a twinkle in my eye. I don't just look happy; I look radiant and filled with joy.

I have another photo of me at four years old. I am frowning and I look angry. The twinkle in my eye has been replaced with a dark, empty look. It reminds me of the look I have seen in the eyes of criminals—full of hatred and defiance.

What happened to me in those three and a half years? What had taken away the twinkle in my eyes and the joyous smile and replaced them with darkness, emptiness, and hatred? The answer: shame. Shame had replaced my innocence, joy, and exuberance for life. Shame had caused me to build up a wall of protection and defiance.

The person I was defending myself against was my mother, a woman who was so full of shame herself that she couldn't help but project it onto me, her unwanted child and the constant reminder of her own shame.

In addition to the neglect and emotional and physical abuse that I suffered at my mother's hands, I was also sexually molested at age nine and raped at age twelve. By the time I was sexually abused I already felt there was something very wrong with me. I felt like a burden and a colossal disappointment to my mother. Once I was sexually abused, those feelings of not being good enough turned into feelings of self-hatred.

The sexual abuse caused me to feel permanently marked—as if everyone could see what an evil, dirty, unacceptable human being I had become. I felt so damaged, so worthless, that I was surprised if someone was kind to me. And because I felt so undeserving of kindness, I either sabotaged relationships or sexualized them.

As it is with many victims of childhood abuse, these experiences from my childhood combined to create a deep, multilayered sense of shame in me, and this sense of shame helped to form my character.

Shame infused every aspect of my life. Because of debilitating shame I have struggled with my weight nearly all my life, and I came seriously close to falling into alcoholism and all that entailed, including risking my own and other people's lives. Because of debilitating shame I became sexually promiscuous, putting myself in dangerous situations and having unprotected sex. And because of debilitating shame I repeated the cycle of abuse by becoming both a continual victim and an abuser.

I have come to realize that discovering how to heal both my own shame and the shame of my clients is my calling. As damaging and debilitating as shame has been in my life, my quest to rid myself of it has led me to wonderful places and incredible people. It led me to my career as a therapist and as an author. It led me to two wonderfully compassionate therapists and introduced me to the practices of restorative justice, nonviolent communication, Buddhism, and mindfulness. And it put me on a path of compassion that led me to the teachings of Alice Miller, Mahatma Gandhi, Martin Luther King, Jr., Nelson Mandela, and the Dalai Lama.

Shame transformed me from an innocent, open, joy-filled six-month-old to a defended, angry, joyless four-year-old; my quest to heal myself of my shame has led me back to that state of joy and open-heartedness. The person I am today is who I was born to be—open, loving, joyous, and filled with loving-kindness. This is who we are all born to be.

I have experienced a lifetime of debilitating shame. While I am not saying that I have rid myself of absolutely all my shame, thanks to compassion and self-compassion the majority is finally gone. How sad that it took a lifetime to accomplish. But this doesn't have to be your experience. I worked long and hard to discover a cure for shame for victims of childhood abuse, and I am happy to say that I found it. I offer it here for you as the greatest gift I can give you.

Part I of this book explores in detail the links between childhood abuse and shame—particularly the patterns of painful and destructive thoughts, feelings, and behaviors abuse victims find themselves locked into due to shame. It also introduces the concept and practice of self-compassion. Part II addresses the obstacles many former victims have to the idea and practice of self-compassion. It offers steps you can take to prepare yourself to begin the practice of self-compassion, including initiating you into ways of thinking and acting that are compatible with self-compassion. Part III outlines the Compassion Cure program and teaches you, step by step, how to accomplish each aspect of it.

There are five components to the Compassion Cure program: (1) self-understanding, (2) self-forgiveness, (3) self-acceptance, (4) self-kindness, and (5) self-encouragement. These components are presented in chapters 7 through 11. It may take you weeks or even months to complete the entire program, since you will want to practice the steps outlined in each of these chapters before moving on to the next. I highly recommend that you complete the exercises, which are designed to help you benefit as much as possible from each component. Readers of my previous books have reported that they got much more out of the books when they took the time to complete the exercises. Some read the book in its entirety and then went back to complete the exercises, while others reported that it worked best for them to complete the exercises as they read each chapter.

Since shame can cause self-destructive behavior such as suicidal thoughts, recklessness, and self-mutilation, it's essential that you seek professional help if you experience any of these symptoms while working through the book.

Part I

The Shame/ Compassion Connection

1 How and Why Child Abuse Creates Shame

Shame is the lie someone told you about yourself.

—Anaïs Nin (attributed)

If you are a survivor of childhood abuse it is very likely that you have continued to suffer negative effects because of it. These effects can include perfectionism, self-criticism, self-neglect, self-destructiveness (self-harm, suicidal attempts), addictions (alcohol, drugs, shopping, gambling, stealing, sex, workaholism), eating disorders, a tendency to sabotage your relationships or career, or a tendency to be abusive or to be involved with abusive partners. It is also likely that you have reached out for help in some way for your problems, perhaps joining a twelve-step program or support group or seeking individual counseling, and you may have received some help. But there is one consequence of childhood abuse that you have probably not been able to alleviate, no matter how much help you've received. This is debilitating shame—one of the biggest obstacles that adult victims of child abuse experience.

As a counselor, my specialty for thirty-five years has been working with adults who were abused as children. I have found that most of my clients suffer from *debilitating shame*: shame so all-consuming that it negatively affects every aspect of a person's life—her perception of herself, her relationships with others, her ability to be intimate with a romantic partner, her ability to risk and achieve success in her career, and her overall physical and emotional health. While everyone experiences shame from time to time, and many have issues related to shame, adult victims of childhood abuse suffer from shame more often and have far more issues related to shame than any other group of people.

This is because shame is a natural reaction to abuse. Abuse is by nature humiliating and dehumanizing. There is a feeling of being invaded and defiled, and the indignity of being helpless and at the mercy of another person. This feeling occurs most profoundly in the case of child sexual abuse, but it occurs with all forms of abuse. For example, physical abuse is not only an assault on the body, it is an insult to the victim's integrity. No one has the right to attack our body—it is a violation. Emotional abuse has been described as "soul murder" (Hirigoyen 2000). Constant criticism, name-calling, belittling, unreasonable expectations, and other forms of emotional abuse can be just as harmful and just as shame-inducing as physical or sexual attacks; some experts, including myself, believe that the negative effects of emotional abuse can last longer and have more far-reaching consequences than other forms of abuse. Neglect can also create shame in a child, causing her to think, "If my own mother doesn't love me enough to take care of me, I must be worthless." How else can a child interpret being neglected or abandoned by a parent?

Victims of childhood abuse also tend to feel shame because, as human beings, we want to believe that we have control over what happens to us. When that is challenged by a victimization of any kind, we feel humiliated. We believe we should have been able to defend ourselves. And because we weren't able to do so, we feel helpless and powerless. This powerlessness leads to humiliation and to shame.

It is especially shaming to a child when a parent abuses her, violating her body and integrity. Physical abuse in particular sends the message that the child is "bad" and therefore "unlovable." Children want to feel loved and accepted by their parents more than anything. And because parental love is so important, children will make up all kinds of excuses for a parent's behavior—even abusive behavior. Most often the child ends up blaming himself for "causing" his parent to abuse him, thinking, "If I had just done what she asked me to she wouldn't have gotten so mad," or "I know I'm a disappointment to my father—no wonder he has to get on me all the time."

Shame: The Most Destructive of Human Emotions

Ask any group of people what they think the most destructive human emotion is, and most would choose anger or fear. But actually, it's shame. Shame is the source of cruelty, violence, and destructive relationships, and is at the core of many addictions. It can damage a person's self-image in ways no other emotion can, causing her to feel deeply flawed, inferior, worthless, unlovable. If someone experiences enough shame he can become so self-loathing that he becomes self-destructive or even suicidal.

Shame is more insidious and all-pervasive than other emotions, and it can be hard to identify. It can take over your body and mind. When you feel shame, it is like someone pricked you with a pin and took out all the air. You feel deflated, diminished, weakened, flattened.

Physically, some describe shame as a burning feeling; others describe becoming flushed and red in the face, or numb—no feeling at all. Still others feel nausea and a pounding heart. Many experience an inability to speak or think and a strong desire to get away.

Shame is a feeling deep within us of being exposed and unworthy. When we feel shamed, we want to hide. It shows in our bodies: we hang our heads, stoop our shoulders, and curve our bodies inward as if trying to become invisible. These physical manifestations are often accompanied with thoughts like "I'm a total failure" or "I'm so stupid." People who have been deeply shamed take on the underlying, pervasive belief that they are defective or unacceptable. They feel unworthy, unlovable, or bad.

Shame can also cause us to feel isolated—set apart from the crowd. In fact, in many cultures historically, people were banished from the group for breaking society's rules. Being shamed feels like being banished—unworthy to be around others.

Shame can also cause us to feel separated from our real selves. As a self-protective measure, we may create elaborate masks—smiling, pleasing others, trying to appear self-confident—in order to cover up our real selves and have others see us as better than we feel we are. As Gershen Kaufman, in his classic book, *Shame: The Power of Caring* (1992), puts it so eloquently, shame is "the affect of indignity, of defeat, of transgression, of inferiority, and of alienation" (xix).

Distinguishing Shame from Guilt

There is little agreement, even among professional therapists, as to the exact difference between guilt and shame (or even if there is a difference). We don't need to get sidetracked in this controversy; for our purposes here's what I consider the most helpful perspective on the issue.

Shame and guilt can feel very similar—with both experiences we feel bad about ourselves. But guilt can be understood as feeling disappointed in oneself for violating an important internal value or code of behavior. With shame, one can also feel a disappointment in oneself, but no value has been violated. As Gershen Kaufman (1992) explains it, "The meaning of the two experiences is as different as feeling inadequate is from feeling immoral" (125).

Some have explained the difference between shame and guilt as follows: When we feel guilt, we feel badly about *something we did or neglected to do*. When we feel shame, we feel badly about *who we are*. Put another way: guilty people fear punishment, shamed people fear abandonment. When we feel guilty we need to learn it's okay to make mistakes. When we feel shame we need to learn it's okay to be who we are.

Another distinction between guilt and shame is that shame comes from public exposure of one's own vulnerability, while guilt is private, coming from a sense of failing to measure up to our own internal standards. When others discover or know we were once helpless, we tend to feel ashamed. We also feel exposed. But if we feel we caused our own problems, we cease to feel vulnerable or exposed to quite the same degree. This can explain why victims of abuse often blame themselves for the abuse. It is easier—less painful—to feel guilt than to feel the shame of helplessness.

Still another difference between guilt and shame is that we don't tend to feel bad about feeling guilty—in fact it's often viewed as a positive thing, especially in terms of how others perceive you. If you feel guilty about what you've done, others are more likely to forgive you. But shame is more taboo—so much so that we actually feel shame about feeling shame. This is partly due to the strong correlation between feeling shame and feeling inferior. We believe we should conceal feelings of shame, especially in a culture that so values achievement and success.

"Victim" or "Survivor"?

In addition to the guilt/shame issue, another controversy needs to be addressed: whether to use the word "victim" or the word "survivor" when describing an adult who was abused as a child. As you may have noticed, I am using the words *victim* or *former victim*; I'll continue to do so through most of the book (changing to *survivor* at the very end). The argument for using the word *survivor* when describing someone who was abused and survived the experience is that this term is more empowering than *victim*, which has the connotation of someone who is weak or damaged. I completely agree that the word *survivor* is much more empowering. But over the years, many clients have told me they're actually offended when someone calls them survivors—especially when their victimization was very recent or when they are just beginning to heal from the abuse.

They've told me they want to be the ones to decide what they call themselves, and that the word *survivor* doesn't fit for them until they have experienced some substantial recovery. An abuse victim may also object to being called "survivor" by others because it feels like her victimization is being glossed over, or that the word *survivor* makes other people more comfortable, while the word *victim* forces them to contend with the fact that she was indeed victimized.

I value this feedback, and it has led me to mostly use the words *victim* or *former victim* to describe adults who were abused as children and who are still in recovery from the abuse. It's not that I don't want you to feel empowered—the word *survivor* can certainly empower. And it's not that I don't give you credit for surviving horrific abuse. It is that I don't want to minimize the abuse that you experienced by avoiding the term *victim*. As an abused child, you were, in fact, a victim, and that has meaning. You were unable to defend yourself or change your circumstances. And as an adult you are very possibly still a victim to the debilitating shame that came with the experience of being abused.

I hope my using this term does not offend you. If you consider yourself a survivor then please substitute that word in your mind whenever I use the term *victim*. I truly respect whatever your choice is. But if you have a strong reaction to the word *victim*, I also ask you to question why that is. Is it possible you are still struggling with the reality that you were, in fact, victimized? If so, is it because deep down inside you are still blaming yourself? Or is it that you hate that someone could overpower you and make you feel like a victim? Considering these possibilities may free you to feel the pain, fear, and anger you felt at the time and can contribute to healing your shame.

In this book you'll meet some of the clients I've worked with over the years. (I have changed their names and identifying details to protect their confidentiality.) These case studies illustrate how the principles and practices I describe in the book helped these people to heal from their debilitating shame. The first story belongs to Emily.

Emily's Story: Debilitating Shame Caused by Emotional and Physical Abuse

Emily came to see me for help with her self-esteem. "I don't feel very good about myself and because of it I let people walk all over me—my husband, people at work, my friends," she said. "I just can't seem to stand up for myself. I even let my kids walk all over me. It's not good for me and I know it's not good for my kids to get their way all the time. They've become so spoiled that no one can stand them."

When I asked Emily why she didn't feel good about herself, she said she didn't really know. "I just don't like myself very much. I don't like the way I look. I've always had a problem with my weight, and I look too much like my mother; I don't like that."

Like Emily, many people seek counseling because they feel they have low self-esteem and believe this is what causes them to be self-critical or to have difficulty standing up for themselves with others, even those who are demanding or abusive. While Emily certainly did suffer from low self-esteem, it was neither the cause of her problem nor even her primary problem. Rather, debilitating shame was at the root of her negative feelings about herself and of her inability to stand up for herself.

Focusing on raising a person's self-esteem doesn't get to the core of the problem, especially when the person has a traumatic background. Emily's mother had been extremely critical and demanding, and had unreasonable expectations of her, insisting that she get all As in school, then come home and keep the house immaculate. Her mother would often force her to do tasks all over again if she wasn't pleased with the result. And she constantly criticized the way Emily looked, yelling at her to stand up straight and scolding her for eating too much: "You're going to end up looking like a pig if you don't stop eating all the time."

After hearing about Emily's history I wasn't surprised that she didn't feel good about herself, that she suffered from poor body image, and that she allowed other people, including her own children, to walk all over her. Emily's mother's treatment of her was extremely shaming.

Interestingly, Emily didn't describe her mother's mistreatment as abuse. In fact, she made excuses for her mother: she was such a taskmaster because she'd grown up in poverty; she wanted Emily to get good grades so she could find a good job; she made her do things over and over because she wanted her to have a good work ethic.

After several sessions, Emily shared with me a time when her mother had become physically violent with her—it was the one time she'd tried standing up to her mother. "I was about twelve years old and I guess I'd been around other kids at school who were assertive, so I thought I'd try it. When my mother told me I needed to polish the silverware all over again because she couldn't see herself in it, I rebelled. I said to her, 'Mother, I did the best I could. Can't you just let it go this one time? I have so much homework to do.'"

Emily remembered clearly what happened next. "My mother's face turned beet red. She leaped up from her chair and walked over to me and slapped my face so hard she knocked me down. Then, as I lay shocked on the floor, she kicked me in the stomach, so hard I almost threw up. 'How dare you talk back to me, you ungrateful little bitch!' she yelled. 'I'll teach you to have a smart mouth!'

"Then she grabbed one of my arms and dragged me to the back door and literally kicked me out of the house. 'You can sleep out in the backyard tonight. Maybe that will remind you of how hard I work to put a roof over your head,' she yelled at the top of her lungs. And that's what I did—I slept outside on one of our chaise lounges all night. It was the dead of winter and I was freezing."

Emily hadn't told me this story to complain about her mother. Nor was she making the connection with why she had a difficult time standing up for herself. Instead, she was letting me know what an obstinate child she had been. She blamed herself for her mother's abusive and shaming treatment of her.

If you are like most victims of childhood abuse, your life has been plagued by debilitating shame, but like Emily, you may not have realized it. Completing the following questionnaire will help you determine whether you are suffering from debilitating shame.

Questionnaire: Do You Suffer from Debilitating Shame Due to Childhood Abuse?

1. Do you blame yourself for the abuse you experienced as a child?

2. Do you believe your parent (or other adult or older child) wouldn't have abused you if you hadn't pushed him or her into doing it?

3. Do you believe you were a difficult, stubborn, or selfish child who deserved the abuse you received?

4. Do you believe you made it difficult for your parents or others to love you?

5. Do you believe you were a disappointment to your parents or family?

6. Do you feel you are basically unlovable?

7. Do you have a powerful inner critic who finds fault with nearly everything you do?

8. Are you a perfectionist?

9. Do you believe you don't deserve to be happy, loved, or successful?

10. Do you have a difficult time believing someone could love you?

11. Do you push away people who are good to you?

12. Are you afraid that if people really get to know you they won't like or accept you? Do you feel like a fraud?

13. Do you believe that anyone who likes or loves you has something wrong with them?

14. Do you feel like a failure in life?

15. Do you hate yourself?

16. Do you feel ugly—inside and out?

17. Do you hate your body?

18. Do you believe that the only way someone can like you is if you do everything they want?

19. Are you a people pleaser?

20. Do you censor yourself when you talk to other people, always being careful not to offend them or hurt their feelings?

21. Do you feel like the only thing you have to offer is your sexuality?

22. Are you addicted to alcohol, drugs, sex, pornography, shopping, gambling, or stealing, or do you suffer from any other addiction?

23. Do you find it nearly impossible to admit when you are wrong or when you've made a mistake?

24. Do you feel bad about the way you've treated people?

25. Are you afraid of what you're capable of doing?

26. Are you afraid of your tendency to be abusive—either verbally, emotionally, physically, or sexually?

27. Have you been in one or more relationships where you were abused either verbally, emotionally, physically, or sexually?

28. Did you or do you feel you deserved the abuse?

29. Do you always blame yourself if something goes wrong in a relationship?

30. Do you feel like it isn't worth trying because you'll only fail?

31. Do you sabotage your happiness, your relationships, or your success?

32. Are you self-destructive (engaging in acts of self-harm, driving recklessly, attempting suicide, and so on)?

33. Do you feel inferior to or less than other people?

34. Do you often lie about your accomplishments or your history in order to make yourself look better in others' eyes?

35. Do you neglect your body, your health, or your emotional needs (not eating right, not getting enough sleep, not taking care of your medical or dental needs)?

There isn't any formal scoring for this questionnaire, but if you answered yes to many of these questions, you can be assured that you are suffering from debilitating shame. If you answered yes to just a few, it is still evident that you have an issue with shame.

Why Is It So Difficult to Heal Shame?

Those who work to help victims of childhood abuse heal know such healing always involves helping their clients address and decrease their shame. But this is easier said than done. While a person may understand intellectually that she didn't cause the victimization, she will still blame herself for it. For example, victims of childhood sexual abuse can be told repeatedly that they were not to blame, yet will still believe they somehow caused the abuse to occur. For many victims, blaming themselves is easier than having to face the fact that the parent, grandparent, sibling, uncle, or aunt they love could sexually abuse them. Other victims are convinced that because the touch or the attention felt good, or because they kept going back to the home of the abuser, it must mean they liked it and that, therefore, they weren't victimized at all, but were willing participants.

Victims of physical abuse often feel they disappointed their parent or other authority figure and thus deserved to be chastised or even beaten. Many of my clients who were severely physically abused argue with me when I call what happened to them "abuse." I've heard everything from "You don't know what a terror I was. My mother could only control me by hitting me with that cord" to "I deserved every beating I got. My father was just trying to teach me to be a man."

For victims of all forms of abuse, in addition to the shame perpetuated by believing the abuse was their fault, there is the shame associated with the violation itself. This is the shame that accompanies feeling powerless and thus humiliated, and the shame that comes from feeling rejected and abandoned by an adult who one loves and desperately wants to be loved by. Facing up to the truth—that they were powerless and helpless or that they were abandoned by someone they loved—is so painful and frightening that many simply refuse to do it.

Often parents believe they need to shame their children into behaving, so they use shaming and humiliation as forms of discipline. They feel they need to break the child's spirit like a cowboy breaks in a horse. But the child ends up growing to hate the parent for her cruelty or becoming terrified of the parent—or both. Either way, the shame the child experiences because of the abuse overwhelms him and becomes part of his character. The child who hates the parent becomes rigid—unable to let in love. He is so filled with shame that he feels that he cannot take in any further shame. He protects himself by making sure he is always "right." Such a person often becomes controlling, shaming, and/or abusive.

The other extreme—the obedient child whose spirit was, in fact, broken—is so hesitant, so reticent, that she cannot step out and take chances. She may become dependent on the abusive parent or on others, and may also be so afraid of being further shamed that she goes along—never questioning authority in any way. She may not be able to speak up when she disagrees with her friends or her partner, and may allow others to walk all over her. (I wrote about this phenomenon in my book *The Nice Girl Syndrome.*) So while shaming is indeed effective in breaking a child's will and spirit, it can be emotionally crippling.

Sometimes a child has been so severely shamed or has experienced so many shame-inducing experiences that he becomes what is referred to as "shame-bound" or "shame-based." He has internalized his shame and it has become a dominant factor in the formation of his personality. Shame-bound people are commonly victims of severe physical discipline, emotional abuse, neglect, and abandonment—which all send the message that the child is worthless, unacceptable, and bad. These abusive acts also convey the message that the adult will treat the child any way he wants because the child is worthless. Many shame-based people were also humiliated for their behavior (being beaten or chastised in front of others; being told things like "What's wrong with you?" or "What would your precious teacher think of you if she knew who you *really* are?").

Shame-bound people don't tend to be those who experienced one type of abuse over a short period. Instead, they either experienced ongoing shame-inducing traumas like sexual abuse throughout their childhood, or their parents severely shamed them from early childhood on. For example, they were taught that they were worthless or bad by hearing adults say such things to them as "You're in my way," "I wish you were never born," or "You'll never amount to anything." Sometimes the words were never actually spoken, but the message conveyed by the parents' behavior or attitude toward the child had the same effect. My mother never told me in words "You are a burden to me" or "You are a disappointment to me," but her actions and attitude spoke volumes. As a consequence of this kind of ongoing shaming, children suffer from extremely low self-esteem, feelings of worthlessness, and self-hatred. They feel inferior, "bad," unacceptable, and different—much like anyone who has been abused and shamed, but to a more intense degree.

Internalized Shame

Internalized shame is experienced as a deep sense of who a person *is*—the feeling that she is defective or never good enough. It becomes the foundation of the self—the feeling around which all other feelings about the self will be experienced. Shame becomes basic to the person's sense of identity.

Internalization also means that the self can activate and experience shame on its own. So you no longer need to be actively shamed (such as experiencing another incident of abuse) in order to feel shamed. In fact, there doesn't need to be any interpersonal shame-inducing event at all. You only need to become triggered by a memory of being shamed, hear self-critical messages inside your head, be reminded of your limitations, think about your failures, or feel rejected or humiliated, and a cascade of shame-based feelings, memories, and perceptions ensues.

Shame-bound people are people who have internalized shame. They live in a constant state of self-criticism and self-blame, or they become exquisitely sensitive to criticism from others and defend against it at every turn. They set unreasonable expectations for themselves and are never satisfied with their performance or achievements. They may find it impossible to take in compliments or even positive expressions of love or admiration from others.

Some shame-bound people withdraw into depression and passivity. These are the people who have truly been "broken" by debilitating shame. Others defend against any feeling of shame with anger. While most people react with anger whenever they are made to feel humiliated, devalued, or demeaned, some shame-bound people tend to be extremely sensitive and defensive, going into rages when they

feel criticized or attacked—which is often. Because they are so critical of themselves they believe everyone else is critical of them. And
because they despise themselves they assume everyone else dislikes
them. If you are shame-bound, one teasing comment or one well-
intentioned criticism can send you into a rage that lasts for hours.
Feeling shamed by the other person, you may spend hours making
the person feel horrible—dumping shame back on her.

Some shame-based people also use anger as a defense by attack-
ing others before they have a chance to attack him. She is in essence
saying, "Don't get any closer to me. I don't want you to know who I
really am." This raging works—it drives people away or keeps people
from approaching in the first place.

Those who defend against shame build up a wall to keep any
hint of criticism from others out. Strategies can include: being critical of others before they have a chance to criticize you, refusing to
talk about your shortcomings, turning criticism around on the other
person, accusing the other person of lying or exaggerating about
their complaints about you, and projecting your shame onto others.

Carrying around debilitating shame is like being weighed down by
a heavy burden. And defending against the shame doesn't make it
disappear—it continues to fester like a wound that won't heal. So how
does one heal debilitating shame from childhood abuse? By facing
your shame, not running from it. As much as it hurts to come out of
denial and face the truth about the abuse and your abuser, it hurts
even more to keep carrying the shame caused by blaming yourself.

Why You Must Heal Your Shame in Order to Heal from Childhood Abuse

After they experience a trauma, especially childhood abuse, shame
can haunt victims in a powerful yet often unrecognized manner. This
shame, often called *trauma-bound shame*, can impair healing and
recovery, causing victims to stay frozen, unable to forgive themselves
for being abused or for what they consider their part in the abuse.

Shame is an emotion that piggybacks on trauma. It complicates the healing and recovery process on many levels, including psychologically (victims blame themselves for being vulnerable) and spiritually (it can change victims' relationship with their higher power). To make matters worse, shame can cause victims to be resistant to reaching out for help for fear of being exposed. Shame is at the core of nearly every symptom victims experience—another reason it must be addressed if there is any real hope for recovery. While there are other aspects of healing from childhood abuse, none is more important than ridding yourself of debilitating shame. Once you have healed from your shame, you'll have more motivation, strength, and energy to tackle other issues.

Once they've successfully faced and eliminated their shame, clients have said:

"I feel like a completely different person, like somehow I've been infused with energy. I feel lighter, more joyful—like I can take on the world!"

"I used to feel like people were always looking at me and being critical. Now I realize the only one who was judging me was me."

"Before I addressed my shame and figured out why I hated myself so much my life was miserable. Now I know that I'm a good person and I deserve to be happy. My life has completely changed."

"I used to sabotage every good relationship, every positive thing that happened to me, because I was so full of shame. Now I recognize it and spend time telling myself I deserve love and success. I don't believe it completely yet—but at least I don't push good things away as much."

"I used to neglect my needs just like my mother did. The shame I felt because she didn't love me was horrendous. But I've gradually come to understand that her treatment of me had nothing to do with who I am. In fact, now I believe I should treat myself especially well because I didn't receive love and caring as a child. What a difference!"

Recovering from the burden of shame, these clients found they felt so much better about themselves that they had more motivation and courage to face other aspects of healing.

The Compassion Cure

I call my program *The Compassion Cure* because the primary tool we will use to help you heal your shame is compassion. Like many poisons, shame has an antidote—something uniquely able to neutralize its toxicity. Compassion is shame's antidote.

It has been said that all abuse is a failure of compassion for self and others. The Compassion Cure program will teach you specific compassionate attitudes and skills that can reverse your tendency to view yourself in a blaming, condemning, self-critical way. If you have built up a defensive wall to protect yourself from further shaming, these attitudes and skills will make it safe for you to face the shaming events of your childhood so you no longer need to defend yourself against them. If your spirit was broken by abuse and shame, the Compassion Cure will help you begin to understand that you did nothing to deserve the abuse and that you do deserve to be treated with respect.

No matter how you've coped with your abuse, this program will teach you how to develop an internal compassionate relationship with yourself. It will also help you understand why you have behaved as you have and to forgive yourself for any negative behaviors you exhibited in response to the abuse—whether alcohol and drug abuse, sexual acting out, self-harm, abusing others, or breaking the law.

When you free yourself from shame, you suddenly see the world much more clearly. Instead of feeling isolated and less than, you feel a part of and equal to. It's as if life welcomes you back.

This book will guide you step by step through the process of healing your shame. My hope is that you begin to feel—by reading my words and feeling my support—that I am with you on your journey. You don't have to face your shame alone.

2

Why Shame Is So Debilitating

Shame is a sickness of the soul.

Silvan Tomkins

John is a sex addict. Unlike most men, who think about sex several times a day, John thinks about sex almost constantly and is driven to have sex several times a day. "I've lost my wife and kids, ruined my career, and lost any vestige of self-respect I once had," he told me during a session. "I put myself into extremely dangerous situations because I'll go anywhere and be with anyone to satisfy my compulsion for sex—especially dangerous or illicit sex. I'm lucky I haven't contracted AIDS or been murdered in a dark alley."

Janice also suffers from an addiction—to alcohol. Before she came to see me she had been in three alcohol treatment facilities in four years. During her last stay in an inpatient facility, she uncovered memories of childhood sexual abuse, and she came to suspect she had been trying to numb herself with alcohol ever since she took her first drink. "I'm tired of relapsing," she said between sobs. "I want to deal with the abuse so I don't have to drink."

Amanda came to see me because she had a problem maintaining good relationships. "I ruin every good relationship I get in—even with friends. If someone is good to me, it won't be long before I push them away somehow. I'll say or do something that is so insulting or hurtful that the other person can't stay with me and still feel good about themselves. I don't ever blame them—I'd walk away from someone like me too. But I'm surrounded by lowlifes—I don't seem to push *them* away. I want to find out what is wrong with me—why I do this."

Brent had been seeing me for quite some time. He came to therapy after discovering he was being emotionally abused by his wife. Ironically, his wife had read my book *The Emotionally Abusive Relationship* because she thought she was the one being abused. She gave the book to Brent to read, and he discovered it was actually he who was the victim. "I can't believe how I allowed my wife to talk to me for so many years, how I let her degrade me and humiliate me. I actually believed what she said; I thought that her perceptions of me were the truth. Now I'm amazed at how differently I see things."

While these people seem to have entirely different problems, they have something important in common that drives them to act the way they do. They all suffer from debilitating shame. They are so overwhelmed with shame that it causes them to behave in self-defeating, self-destructive ways. Each was abused in some way in childhood—another commonality they all share. But it's the shame they experienced at having been abused that drives them to act in such unhealthy ways.

John was sexually abused by his grandfather starting when he was five and continuing until he was ten. The shame John feels because of the abuse and the circumstances surrounding it haunts him every day. "I wake up hating myself. I hate my body; I hate my penis. I hate everything about myself. I've done nothing but bring pain and disruption to everyone I've ever loved—starting with my grandmother. When she found out what my grandfather and I were doing she was so disgusted she kicked him out of the house. And she couldn't even look me in the eyes after that, she despised me so much. My whole family adored my grandfather and they all blamed me because he wasn't allowed to come to our house any longer—not even for holidays. If they wanted to see him they had to meet him away from the house and away from me."

It did no good to tell John that the sexual abuse was not his fault, that he wasn't responsible for his grandparents' divorce or his grand-father's banishment. It wasn't his fault that his good Grandpa—the man he had once adored—spent holidays alone and ended up dying alone in a little apartment. John felt so responsible for everything that happened—the abuse itself and the aftermath once it was revealed—that my words alone weren't going to help him understand he was an innocent victim. It didn't help that his family silently blamed John for the loss of their beloved grandfather, or that John as a young boy had acted out the sexual abuse he had suffered by introducing his cousins and several neighborhood children to sex. John's shame surrounding the sexual abuse was overwhelming, and exacerbated by the fact that he now felt driven to act out the shame every day of his life.

Janice was also sexually abused, but instead of being driven to reenact the abuse the way John was, she tried to ward off the memories of abuse by numbing herself with alcohol. "It's the only way I can stop myself from thinking about it. When I'm not drunk, I have continual flashbacks that are so horrible I can't stand it."

Janice's experience could rightly be described more as torture than abuse. Her father, her abuser, was sadistic, and he added an element of humiliation to nearly every sexual act he performed on her, whether it was calling her horrible names during the sexual act, urinating on her, or stimulating her clitoris to the point where she would have an orgasm and then laughing and telling her no one would ever satisfy her the way he did. This sadistic humiliation added to the shame Janice already felt due to her loss of control at being victimized and to the secrecy involved in keeping the abuse from the rest of her family.

Amanda's pattern of pushing people away reminded me of my own, so I felt an immediate rapport with her. Just as it had been with me, Amanda pushed people away because she didn't believe she deserved good things. She had been emotionally abused by her mother, overtly and deliberately. It seemed that Amanda's mother was determined to destroy her daughter's confidence.

From the time Amanda was a little girl her mother made fun of her—of how she looked and talked, and especially of her attempts to accomplish something. When she begged her mother to let her go to dance school, she said, "Don't waste your time and my money. You're too fat and clumsy to be a dancer." And anytime someone complimented Amanda, her mother would negate the compliment with comments like "Oh, don't let her fool you, she isn't the sweet little thing she pretends to be; she's really a devil." Comments like these were hurtful and embarrassing to Amanda, and they made her doubt herself: maybe her mother was right, she would think—maybe she really was a bad person

Brent's wife's abusive, shaming behavior only added to the shame he already felt due to the fact that both his parents continually verbally and physically abused him as a child. In fact, it was because he had been abused and shamed in childhood that he married his wife—a controlling, critical person who was as hard to please as his parents. Someone with a healthier childhood would have walked away at the first signs of his wife's critical, controlling behavior, but not only was Brent accustomed to being treated in this manner, he was unconsciously attempting to relive his childhood trauma in hopes of getting things right this time. This is a very common pattern; Freud called it the *repetition compulsion*. The problem was that instead of undoing his trauma through repetition, Brent added to it. He was so full of shame from childhood that each time his wife accused him of not being good enough or not trying hard enough, he heard his parents' words echoing in his ear. And as it had been with them, he could never please his wife, no matter how hard he tried. By the time Brent came into therapy with me he was a shell of a man, feeling so much like a failure that he had little motivation to even try to make the changes to his life necessary to end the abusive relationship.

These clients represent just four examples of how shame creates havoc and devastation in abuse victims' lives. There are many others. In this chapter I will describe various ways shame manifests itself in the lives of victims of childhood abuse, and explore more deeply what we know about the emotion of shame itself.

The Many Layers of Shame

Being victimized is in itself a shaming experience, given the humiliation that comes from being violated and the loss of control experienced because of it. In cases where a child has been physically or emotionally abused under the guise of "discipline" or "punishment" by an authority figure, there is the added shame of her being made to feel like she is a disappointment to the adult.

Projection can also be an aspect of shaming in childhood abuse. Most abusers are projecting their own shame onto their victims when they abuse them. In fact, that is often the abuser's motivation, however unconscious. This was very clear in the examples of Janice and Amanda. Janice's father had suffered his own horrendous experiences with sadistic sexual abuse, and he projected the resulting shame onto his daughter. In other words, he could not contain the amount of shame he felt, so it spilled out onto her. Amanda's mother had also been shamed in childhood, in the very same ways she shamed Amanda. Amanda described her grandmother as a strict taskmaster who seemed to enjoy putting people down.

A further source of shame is when the abuse has been exposed. This experience of shame is perhaps most acute in cases of sexual abuse. As shaming as the experience of sexual abuse can be in itself, its exposure can be just as shaming, depending upon the reactions of significant others. In John's case, his grandmother's reaction was particularly shaming, since she made it clear by her comments and her attitude that she blamed John for the abuse. In fact, she treated him like he had somehow enticed his grandfather into molesting him. As if that wasn't enough, his parents and other family members blamed him because his grandfather was forbidden by law to set foot in the family home again (he and his parents were living in the home of his grandparents when the abuse occurred). The family spoke openly about how sad it was that Grandpa lived all alone and about how much they missed him. Instead of helping John heal from the terrible shame of the abuse, his family's actions and attitudes compounded his burden of shame.

Other victims are shamed by the reactions of those to whom they make their outcry. Not being believed can add to the victim's shame, especially if the person a child tells about the abuse interrogates the child or gets angry at the child for telling. When I first told my mother about being molested, she didn't believe me. Since she had already decided I was a liar, she assumed I was making it up to "get attention." This added to the shame and humiliation I already felt as the result of the abuse.

Some parents or other caretakers shame the child by saying he falsely accused the perpetrator, making the child feel as if he is now the offender, victimizing an innocent person. When John's abuse was finally exposed—a teacher took him aside to talk after noticing how depressed he was—his grandmother and his parents all rallied around his grandfather, saying, "How could you lie like this about such a sweet old man who has always been so good to you?"

Victims may also experience horrible shame when they have to talk to police and other authorities. And if the child ends up going to court, this can engender still further shame. Shame makes us feel *exposed*—seen in a painfully diminished way. The more a child has to tell the story of the abuse, the more exposed she can feel. Conversely, some victims feel relieved of the burden of shame when they make an outcry, since holding secrets can add to our shame. (We'll talk about shame and secrets later.)

Finally, there is the shame that victims experience due to the ways in which they tried to cope with the abuse. We see this most acutely in John's case, since he began reenacting his own abuse with other children soon after his grandfather began abusing him. In Janice's situation, not only did she suffer from the shame created by her father's sadistic abuse, but she experienced the shame of having become an alcoholic and of "failing" three stints in rehab. Amanda had the shame of realizing she had hurt so many people in her life, pushing away every person who had been good to her, sometimes cruelly. Brent suffered the humiliation so many adults who are physically or emotionally abused by their mates feel—the shame at having stayed in an abusive relationship for so long. He also experienced the added shame of having been a male victim of emotional abuse, a situation few people really understand or sympathize with.

So it's important to realize there are many layers of shame experienced due to childhood abuse:

⊛ The shame and humiliation that come from the violation itself and from feeling so helpless and powerless

⚜ The shame felt when a child feels she is a disappointment to her parent or other authority figure

⚜ The shame we take on when the abuser projects his shame onto us

⚜ The shame that can come from having the abuse exposed

⚜ The shame that comes from our attempts to cope with our burden of shame, whether through addiction, self-harm, abusing others, or other destructive means

When we realize how many potential layers there are to shame, it makes sense that it can be difficult to heal, and that healing will take time, patience, and understanding.

Shame Is Not a Singular Experience

While it's true that shame due to childhood abuse doesn't have a single source, it's also true that it's not a singular experience. Rather, it is a cluster of feelings and experiences. These can include:

Feelings of being humiliated. Abuse is always humiliating to the victim, but some types are more humiliating than others. Certainly, sexual abuse almost always has an element of humiliation to it, since it is a violation of very private body parts and since there is a knowing on the child's part that incest and/or sex between a child and an adult is taboo. (These taboos hold in nearly every culture in the world.) If the abuse involves public exposure—for example, being chastised or physically punished in front of others, particularly peers—the element of humiliation can be quite profound.

Feelings of impotence. When a child realizes there is nothing he can do to stop the abuse, he feels powerless, helpless. This can also lead to his always feeling unsafe, even long after the abuse has stopped.

Feelings of being exposed. Abuse and the accompanying feelings of vulnerability and helplessness cause the child to feel self-conscious and exposed—seen in a painfully diminished way. The fact that he could not stop the abuse makes him feel weak and exposed both to himself and to anyone present.

Feelings of being defective or less-than. Most victims of abuse report feeling defective, damaged, or corrupted following the experience of being abused.

Feelings of alienation and isolation. What follows the trauma of abuse is the feeling of suddenly being different, less-than, damaged, or cast out. And while victims may long to talk to someone about their inner pain, they often feel immobilized, trapped, and alone in their shame.

Feelings of self-blame. Victims almost always blame themselves for being abused and being shamed. This is particularly true when abuse happens or begins in childhood.

Feelings of rage. Rage almost always follows having been shamed. It serves a much-needed self-protective function of both insulating the self against further exposure and actively keeping others away.

Fear, hurt, distress, or rage can also accompany or follow shame experiences as secondary reactions. For example, feeling exposed is often followed by fear of further exposure and further occurrences of shame. Rage protects the self against further exposure. And along with shame, a victim can feel intense hurt and distress from having been abused.

The following exercise can help you discover what your primary feeling experiences of shame are.

Exercise: Your Feeling Experience of Shame

While you may have experienced all the feelings listed above, you may resonate with some more than others. Think about each type of abuse that you suffered and the various feelings that accompanied it. Ask yourself which of the items listed above stand out to you the most for each type of abuse, or each experience of abuse. In my case, for example, when I think about the sexual abuse I suffered at age nine, I resonate most profoundly with *defectiveness, isolation, self-blame, and rage.*

The Effects of Shame

While all forms of abuse create shame in victims, some victims experience far more shame than others and are affected by the shame they experience more than others. The nature and severity of shame's effects can depend on these factors:

- The importance to the victim of the person who is doing the abusing and shaming

- Whether the victim is shamed publicly or privately

- The number of times the abuse and shaming is repeated

- Whether the victim had emotional support (another caring adult, a sibling who was also experiencing abuse, even a pet)

- The capacity of the victim to cope effectively with both the shaming experience and the emotion of shame itself

For example, being abused and shamed at the hands of a stranger may create less shame than abuse and shaming at the hands of a parent. Also, public humiliation can create a deeper wound than the same action done in private; for example, if a child is scolded in front of her peers it can be far more humiliating than if she were scolded in private.

I find it useful to divide the effects of shame into two broad categories: severe and moderate.

Severe Effects of Shame

Severe effects—the most debilitating and powerful ones—can be experienced alone or can sometimes overlap and merge into one another. They include:

❀ Feelings of self-hatred and self-loathing: can include feeling disgust with oneself or with one's body, and feeling undeserving of any good—including love, affection, success, or happiness. This self-hatred can lead to self-sabotaging behaviors and to self-destructiveness.

❀ Self-destructiveness: may include thoughts of self-harm or actual self-harm or self-mutilation, such as cutting or burning. It also includes thoughts of suicide or actual suicide attempts. Victims are often more generally self-destructive in other ways as well, engaging in dangerous activities such as unprotected sex, reckless driving, driving while intoxicated or under the influence of drugs, extreme sports, associating with dangerous people, or engaging in criminal behavior.

❀ Self-neglect: includes not providing for oneself the basic human needs such as adequate food or proper nutrition, water, clothing and shelter, and rest and sleep. It also includes not taking care of one's dental and medical needs.

❀ Reenacting childhood abuse: can include becoming involved with partners or friends who are replicas of one's abusers— sometimes even choosing someone who looks like the abuser. It can also include becoming like one's abusers (taking on their mannerisms, speech, and behaviors) and passing on the abuse to others (usually romantic partners and children). And it can include developing a pattern of allowing others to abuse you (emotionally, physically, or sexually) or allowing others to take advantage of you.

❀ Addictive behavior: includes developing addictions to alcohol, drugs, sex, pornography, shopping, stealing, gambling, love, and other addictions.

❀ Rage: can be manifested in bitterness, hostility, and abuse toward others if projected outward. If held in and directed at oneself rage can lead to depression, self-hatred, self-harm, and self-punishment (see first two items, above).

❀ Isolation: remaining isolated from others is often motivated by an unconscious or conscious rationale, such as "If I'm not around other people, I don't risk being further abused or shamed." Isolating patterns include feeling extremely anxious about socializing with others, being unable or unwilling to socialize with others, remaining closed up in one's home and seldom going out, and/or remaining withdrawn—being unable to strike up conversations or respond to overtures from others.

Moderate Effects of Shame

While these effects do not generally bring as much devastation into the lives of victims of child abuse as their more severe counterparts, they can still be extremely painful and difficult to overcome, and can affect victims' lives in significant ways. These include:

❀ Sensitivity to correction or criticism: being easily shamed

❀ Defensiveness: creating a wall between oneself and others; blocking out criticism

❀ Tendency to be self-critical, harsh with oneself, unforgiving of oneself

❀ Perfectionism, in an attempt to avoid further shaming

❀ People-pleasing behavior, in an attempt to avoid further shaming and abuse

❀ An inability to speak up for oneself or say what one really means out of fear of offending or hurting someone else, thus risking further shaming

❀ A drive to be successful and/or powerful, in an attempt to gain control over others

❀ Lack of motivation (inability to follow through on set goals and plans); confusion (inability to discover a career path or commit to a partner)

✿ Unreasonably high expectations of oneself and others

You've probably recognized some of your own behavioral patterns and ways of thinking as you've read this chapter, but the following exercise can help you clarify and reflect on them further.

Exercise: How Has Debilitating Shame Affected You?

1. Look over the lists of the severe and moderate effects of shame, noticing which items apply to you. Put a check mark next to these items. Note that you may experience effects on both lists.

2. Pay attention to how you feel as you do this assessment. You may already be aware of the ways shame has affected you, so this might feel like a validating experience for you. Or you may not have come to the realization that the emotion of shame is what has caused you to experience these feelings and behaviors. It can feel liberating to finally make sense of what in the past seemed to you (and others) to be unexplainable behavior. It can also feel good to realize that you are not alone in these patterns. However, feelings of sadness and anger may arise as you come to realize concretely to what extent the abuse and the accompanying shame have affected your life. If you can, just allow yourself to feel these emotions without becoming overwhelmed by them. I'll provide help in later chapters on how to accomplish this.

Defending Against Shame

Everyone experiences shame when we feel exposed or humiliated. Normally, people feel the emotion of shame and then allow it to pass on. But victims tend to internalize shame. The only way a person can survive the kind of intolerable shame that occurs with childhood neglect and abuse is to take on *defensive strategies*. These are created to protect the self from feeling completely overwhelmed with shame, and to protect against further exposure and further experiences of shame. When a child is deeply shamed, he can turn this shame against himself or against others. It is important to recognize that this decision to take on the shame and then either keep it turned inward or turn it against others is an unconscious one and is informed by many factors, including the child's sex, temperament, family role modeling, and culture. For example, extroverted children are more likely to express rage after being shamed, while introverted children will tend to keep the rage inside. Introverted children are also more prone to internal withdrawal (Kaufman 1992).

Passive Strategies

Examples of defensive strategies in which the person turns the shame inward include:

- ✿ Internal withdrawal: withdrawing deeper inside oneself in order to escape the pain of exposure or rejection; engaging in internal fantasy or daydreams to gain positive feelings about the self; "checking out" emotionally and staying disconnected from the outside world.

- ✿ Escaping and isolating behaviors: keeping one's distance from others; seeking out private, secure places where one can be alone and unseen; avoiding social situations; avoiding intimacy.

- ✿ Pretending or people-pleasing behaviors: hiding one's true feelings; being overly submissive and nonassertive; putting the needs of others first; putting up a false front (pretending to be more self-confident or more comfortable than one actually is).

- ✿ Perfectionism: attempting to avoid further shaming by never making mistakes; being overly self-critical; setting unreasonable expectations of oneself.

❀ Self-blame: blaming oneself whenever anything goes wrong. May have learned that if one is quick enough to blame oneself, one can sometimes avoid being blamed by others. Congruent with the thought processes of traumatized people who search for faults in their own behavior in an effort to make sense out of what happened to them.

❀ Comparison: constantly comparing oneself to others and always feeling less-than.

Aggressive Strategies

Examples of defensive strategies in which the person copes by turning shame outward include:

❀ Rage (directed outward): becoming belligerent and aggressive as a self-protective strategy; becoming enraged over the slightest perceived affront to oneself or one's dignity; hostility and bitterness toward others.

❀ Contempt: being judgmental, critical, or condescending toward others; defending oneself against shame by believing that one is better than others—needing to feel superior to avoid being submerged in feelings of inferiority.

❀ Striving for power and control: attempting to compensate for the sense of defectiveness that underlies internalized shame. The more powerful one is, the less vulnerable one becomes to further shaming.

❀ Transferring blame: making someone else feel shame in order to reduce one's own shame.

❀ Identifying with the aggressor: by becoming like one's abuser, taking on his qualities and defending him, one can suppress the feelings of helplessness that are so difficult to face (especially for male victims). By doing to others what was done to you, you discharge both shame and aggression.

All these strategies serve to temporarily alleviate the painful feelings of inadequacy, inferiority, and unlovability that shame-bound people struggle with. None of them actually address the root cause of shame.

The following exercise can help you consciously identify the types of defenses against debilitating shame you took on.

Exercise: Which Defensive Strategies Did You Take On?

Go back over the types of defensive strategies listed above and find the ones that apply to you. How did you react to the abusive or shaming experiences in your childhood? Most people take on several strategies, and many can actually function together. And while you may notice that most of your defensive strategies fall into one category—either aggressive or passive—don't be surprised if you took on a mixture of strategies.

Please do not criticize yourself for the strategies you have used to cope with your shame. Remember that whatever strategies you have used, whatever behaviors you have exhibited, were for the purpose of taking care of yourself and protecting yourself from further shaming. Shame is such a devastating emotion that one has to find a strategy for keeping it at bay.

An Ongoing Process

Recognizing how shame has affected you is an ongoing process. Even though I consider myself an expert on the subject of shame, I've been surprised to suddenly realize it was shame that caused a certain behavior or way of thinking about myself. As those layers of shame I talked about earlier are exposed and peeled away, we are often confronted with yet another layer that had gone unrecognized. For example, as I have gotten older I have developed more of a tendency to spend time alone, even though I have an outgoing personality. I didn't really view this as a problem, particularly since I connect so deeply with my clients and recognize that I need time alone to recuperate. And I also need lots of alone time as an author. I certainly did not view my solitary lifestyle as a result of shame.

Yet recently when I met a friend for dinner I noticed I felt differently than I normally do in that situation. I didn't know what it was at first, but then I realized I wasn't holding my body as tightly as I typically would. At first I didn't connect my being more relaxed with having less shame, but then I was able to make the connection: being out socially, even with a friend, was stressful to me. Although I wasn't consciously thinking about it, whenever I put myself out there socially I was risking being shamed.

I had recently been doing some further healing work on my shame using self-compassion, and this episode showed me I was experiencing positive results. Now that I had healed another layer of my shame, I felt less afraid of being exposed, and I was more relaxed with my friend than I had been in the past. I'm certain there will be more layers to discover and heal (or heal and then discover, as in this case!), but each time I progress I feel better about myself.

In addition to carefully reviewing your responses to the exercises in this chapter, this might be a time for you to recognize any progress you have made in healing from your shame. What triggers have lost their power? What defenses no longer seem so very vital? You may realize, as I did, that you no longer have a particular symptom. Give yourself credit for your progress. Acknowledge your healing, and above all feel proud of yourself. Please remember: while compassion is the antidote to shame, healthy pride is shame's polar opposite. The more pride you can have in yourself and your progress, the more good feelings you will have about yourself, and this in itself can help alleviate your shame.

As you continue to face the truth about how shame has affected your life, take care not to shame yourself for feeling shame. It can be painful to realize how much shame has devastated your life, and it is important to feel that pain. But don't put yourself down. Remember that *every* person who was abused in childhood was shamed and that all of us have been affected by that shame in some way. You can't help or change the fact that shame has caused you to behave in certain ways any more than you can help or change the fact that you were abused. If you realize that shame has caused you to have many unhealthy ways of coping, *don't blame yourself for it.* You are doing the best you can to cope with a very difficult and painful situation. As destructive as your ways of coping may be, they are just that—ways of coping—and they have helped you survive the abuse and shaming you experienced.

As you reflect on the sources of your shame and the means you've taken to cope with it, please don't compare yourself with others who have been abused. It may seem to you that others don't have as many negative behaviors as you do, or aren't as debilitated by the struggle with shame as you are. But you don't really know that for a fact, even if you are comparing yourself to someone you know well, or someone who shares your history of abuse—a sibling, for example. Things are almost never as they appear on the surface. The person you're comparing yourself to may appear to be coping quite well, when in reality she is suffering as much as you are, or even more, but is able to hide her suffering and her symptoms well.

3 How Compassion Can Heal the Shame of Childhood Abuse

Compassion is the radicalism of our time.

—The Dalai Lama

"I hate to talk about my childhood. It doesn't really help. I just end up feeling depressed. Every time I think about how my father treated me I feel so small and inadequate. I hate that feeling. I've worked a long time to get past it so I can hold my head up high and look people in the eye. When I was a kid I walked around with my head down, feeling like there was something so horribly wrong with me— like I didn't deserve to even be around other people. Now I feel confident and proud of myself. I know I'm as good as everyone else."

These were the words of my new client, Martin. Martin had an air of confidence and power about him, like someone used to commanding attention. He looked to be in his late thirties.

"So why have you chosen to come to therapy?" I asked.

"I guess because no matter how hard I try I can't get rid of the image of my father standing over me telling me what a terrible son I am, what a disappointment I am. It's like I'm still living my life to prove to him that I'm not who he said I was. But the sad thing is that no matter how many awards I receive, how much money I make, how successful I am, and how many people look up to me, it all gets wiped away when those images come into my head. I know it sounds like a contradiction—I just said that I now feel good about myself, and I do most of the time. But when those images come into my head they are so powerful they wipe everything else away."

In chapters 1 and 2, I explained how abuse causes victims to feel helpless and powerless, and how these feelings can lead to feeling humiliated, which leads in turn to shame. It may seem that since the feelings of helplessness and/or powerlessness cause victims to feel shamed, that becoming empowered can heal the shame. And this is what many former victims, like Martin, attempt. They believe that if they become powerful, whether by being successful, gaining power over others, or becoming physically powerful, they will no longer feel helpless or powerless and thus will rid themselves of the shame they felt at being overpowered as a child.

Small children go through a stage of development where they feel they can do anything and they won't get hurt. Thus, we see little boys and girls in capes standing on top of furniture and leaping off; standing in front of a make-believe classroom "lecturing" to their students; or getting up in front of a real group of people and singing, doing magic tricks, or performing a skit with no sense of fear or embarrassment. Childhood abuse can wipe this feeling of omnipotence away from a child very quickly.

Many victims of childhood abuse try to recapture the feeling of omnipotence they felt before the abuse by shoring themselves up with walls of defenses, attempting to take back the feeling of control they once had. Thus, we see the child who was emotionally abused by his mother growing up to emotionally abuse his wife and children; the boy who was physically abused by his father becoming a bully toward other children at school; the girl who was sexually abused growing up to be a stripper, fooling herself that in this way she can have power over men. In all these situations, as with Martin, the shame has not been healed—it has just been covered up with bravado or grandiosity.

Building up a defensive wall doesn't keep out the shame. It is still there, just under the surface, and can easily be triggered by a memory (such as Martin's image of his father), by someone's words or actions, by a setback or failure of some kind, or by a rejection. Then suddenly all the shame comes rushing in as if the floodgates have lifted.

Gaining personal power cannot heal the debilitating shame from childhood abuse. The truth is, one cannot be truly empowered until the shame is brought out, examined, and healed by compassion. When I explained this to Martin, he said, "But I want to forget about the abuse. I don't want to bring it all back and examine it. It's bad enough that I have these sudden flashes of my father. I don't want to spend time and money to deliberately bring it all back."

I assured Martin that I understood. That I knew that deliberately bringing it all back seemed counterproductive as well as painful. But I also assured him that he wouldn't be doing it alone; that I would be with him every step along the way and would teach him techniques and ways of thinking that would help him face the abuse and his shame in a much different way. I also reminded Martin that his way of dealing with his shame wasn't working too well.

"Yes, and I haven't told you the half of it. The truth is, I'm not just haunted by memories—I've caught myself beginning to act like my father with my own children." Martin put his hands up to his face as if he were trying to hide. "The first time I couldn't believe it was actually happening. I heard my father's words coming out of my mouth—almost as if I was possessed by him. My son had been doing poorly in math, but we had been working on it together. I thought he was improving, but when he brought home his report card and he got a D in math, I blew up. I couldn't help it—all of a sudden I was yelling at him, saying horrible things. I told him how disappointed I was in him, what a failure he was. I said things like, 'I'm just wasting my time with you. You think I don't have better things to do than spend it spoon-feeding you information you should be smart enough to get on your own? What's wrong with you? Are you just stupid? I can't believe you're my son.'"

Martin looked at me imploringly, "Can you help me so I don't do to my son what was done to me? Can you help me get past this so I don't hurt my boy the way I was hurt?"

"Yes, I can help you," I answered confidently.

Martin broke down and cried. "Okay, I'll do what you suggest. I'll do anything so I don't become my father."

I would venture to say that if you are reading this book it's likely you feel the same way—that you'll do anything to rid yourself of debilitating shame and to break the cycle of abuse, whether it's by making sure you don't become like your abuser or making sure you don't continue to be a victim. Like Martin, you may have already begun to witness behavior in yourself that is too reminiscent of how your abuser acted. Or you may have noticed a pattern forming of your continuing to be abused by others, even into adulthood. Or you may have discovered you're treating yourself the way your abuser treated you—yet another version of repeating the cycle of abuse—one that gets far less attention than the other two but is equally destructive. For example, many former victims of verbal abuse end up repeating to themselves the very same critical messages that their abusive parents told them. Those who were neglected as children may not even know how to take care of themselves, or feel they are worthy of self-care. Thus, they end up neglecting themselves in the same way their parents neglected them, whether by not eating healthy food, eating inadequate amounts of food, not practicing proper hygiene, or neglecting their medical and/or dental needs. If you were abused or neglected as a child and have identified yourself as someone who is affected by debilitating shame, you're at risk of repeating the cycle of abuse. That is why you need to actively work to exorcise the shame from your mind, heart, and body—from your very soul. I believe the best way—perhaps the only way—to do this is to bathe yourself in healing compassion.

How Compassion Cures Shame

Compassion soothes our hurts and comforts our pain. It neutralizes shame's persistent poison. When someone shows compassion toward a person afflicted with shame, they're offering a healing elixir. Even an understanding look, a sigh, or a comforting touch can communicate that the other person is *with us in our pain*. The word *compassion* comes from the Latin roots *com* (with) and *pati* (suffer), so it denotes "suffering with" another person. When a person offers us genuine compassion, he joins us in our suffering.

And when someone joins us in our suffering, she provides us with not one, but five healing gifts:

1. She lets us know she sees us and recognizes our suffering. One of the most powerful needs for humans is to *be seen*. This is especially true for victims of childhood neglect and abuse, who often felt invisible within their families and whose needs were often ignored. When someone offers us compassion, she gives us the gift of seeing us and recognizing our pain.

2. He lets us know he *hears us*. Being heard is another primal need for humans. Again, it is a need that often goes unmet for victims of childhood neglect and abuse, whose expressions of need, want, and feeling often go unheard. Being heard is another healing gift.

3. She confirms to us that we are suffering and that we have a right to express our pain, sadness, fear, anger, or any other emotion due to our suffering. In other words, she *validates* or confirms our experience of suffering. She doesn't deny, minimize, ignore, or otherwise invalidate it, which is what we grew accustomed to when we were children and what we continue to expect, making validation an unexpected and profound healing gift.

4. He lets us know he cares about us as human beings; that he cares about the fact that we suffered and are suffering. Respect and care for our humanity may have been in short supply when we were children, and it is a gift to have this birthright restored to us.

5. She offers us comfort and soothing in some way, whether it's a healing glance, a loving touch, a supportive hug, or kind words. The gift of comforting and soothing stimulates the soothing/contentment system and provides a sense of security that helps tone down negative emotions.

The value of compassion—and its power as an antidote and balm to shame—is clear.

If compassion is the ability to feel and connect with the suffering of another human being, self-compassion is the ability to feel and connect with *one's own suffering*. More specifically for our purposes, self-compassion is the act of extending compassion to one's self in instances of perceived inadequacy, failure, or general suffering. If we are to be self-compassionate, we need to give ourselves the same five gifts we offer to another person toward whom we are feeling compassionate. In other words, we need to offer ourselves the *recognition*, *validation*, and *support* we would offer a loved one who is suffering.

Kristin Neff, a professor of psychology at the University of Texas at Austin, is the leading researcher in the growing field of self-compassion. In her book *Self-Compassion* (2011), she defines self-compassion as "being open to and moved by one's own suffering, experiencing feelings of caring and kindness toward oneself, taking an understanding, nonjudgmental attitude toward one's inadequacies and failures, and recognizing that one's experience is part of the common human experience" (224).

Self-compassion encourages us to begin to treat ourselves and talk to ourselves with the same kindness, caring, and compassion we would show a good friend or a beloved child. Just as connecting with the suffering of others has been shown to comfort and heal, connecting with our own suffering will do the same. If you are able to feel compassion toward others, you can learn to feel it for yourself; the following exercise will show you how.

Exercise: Becoming Compassionate Toward Yourself

1. Think about the most compassionate person you have known—someone kind, understanding, and supportive of you. It may have been a teacher, a friend, a friend's parent, a relative. Think about how this person conveyed his or her compassion toward you and how you felt in this person's presence. Notice the feelings and

sensations that come up with this memory. If you can't think of someone in your life who has been compassionate toward you, think of a compassionate public figure, or even a fictional character from a book, a film, or television.

2. Now imagine that you have the ability to become as compassionate toward yourself as this person has been toward you (or you imagine this person would be toward you). How would you treat yourself if you were feeling overwhelmed with sadness or shame? What kinds of words would you use to talk to yourself?

This is the goal of self-compassion: to treat yourself the same way the most compassionate person you know would treat you—to talk to yourself in the same loving, kind, supportive ways this compassionate person would talk to you. In the following chapters I will offer you more in-depth self-compassion tools and strategies. These will help you decrease or eliminate the shame that has plagued your life.

The Benefits of Practicing Self-Compassion

By learning to practice self-compassion you will also be able to begin doing the following:

⊛ Truly acknowledge the pain you suffered and in so doing, begin to heal

⊛ Take in compassion from others

⊛ Reconnect with yourself, including reconnecting with your emotions

⊛ Gain an understanding as to why you have acted out in negative and/or unhealthy ways

⊛ Stop blaming yourself for your victimization

- ❀ Forgive yourself for the ways you attempted to cope with the abuse

- ❀ Learn to be deeply kind toward yourself

- ❀ Create a nurturing inner voice to replace your critical inner voice

- ❀ Reconnect with others and become less isolated

I hope I have been able to convey to you how compassion and self-compassion can help heal you of your shame. But it is difficult to adequately explain this concept in one chapter. As you continue reading the book and practicing the exercises you will grow to more fully understand what a powerful healer compassion can be.

Groundbreaking Self-Compassion Research

While many spiritual traditions have long stressed the importance of compassion for our well-being and good relations with other people, it's been only recently that researchers have proven compassion can help us in a wide variety of ways, including helping us cope with failure, take risks, and weather criticism and conflicts. It can become a focus for our self-identity, and help us connect to a caring, soothing aspect of our mind so that we can face and cope with life's tragedies (Gilbert 2009). Research has also shown that the way we relate to *ourselves*—whether we regard ourselves kindly or critically, in a friendly and affectionate way or hostilely—can have a major influence on our ability to get through life's difficulties and create within ourselves a sense of well-being.

There has been a great deal of research showing the benefits of self-compassion, including how it can play a major role in alleviating shame. I referred to several of these studies in the introduction. Here I'll focus on those studies that show how self-compassion can benefit trauma victims in their healing.

Not only can shame create a vulnerability to mental health problems, but it also affects the expression of symptoms, abilities to reveal painful information, various forms of avoidance (for example, dissociation and denial), and problems with help-seeking (Gilbert and Procter 2006).

Following trauma, trauma-related cues may trigger fear in an individual, which in turn, may elicit avoidance behaviors. Individuals high in self-compassion will be less likely to feel threatened by—and therefore avoid—painful thoughts, memories, and emotions. Instead, they may be more likely to experience a natural process of exposure to trauma-related stimuli (Thompson and Waltz 2008). In other words, the more self-compassionate you become, the easier it will be to face the trauma of your abusive childhood so you can heal your shame. Other recent findings include:

- Self-compassion can help people prepare themselves for the tasks required in psychotherapy. Higher self-compassion is associated with greater willingness to engage in painful thoughts and emotions and with a lower need to avoid painful experiences (Leary et al. 2007, Neff et al. 2007).

- Self-compassion has been associated with greater resilience— the ability to recover quickly from trauma, illness, change or misfortune. Resilience has also been defined as having the capacity to withstand stress and catastrophe (Neff and McGehee 2010).

- Most important for our purposes, research results show that trauma survivors, particularly those with PTSD, benefit from incorporating elements of self-compassion into treatment. The practice of self-compassion has been shown to decrease post-traumatic symptoms, including self-criticism, depression, thought suppression, anxiety, and rumination. Most victims and abusers alike were emotionally, physically, or sexually abused in childhood and consequently, many suffer from PTSD (Thompson and Waltz 2008).

- A number of therapies now focus on the importance of helping people develop inner compassion and self-soothing abilities. Compassionate Mind Training (CMT) evolved from working with high shame and self-critical people whose problems tend to be chronic, and who find self-warmth and self-acceptance difficult and/or frightening. Results show significant reductions in depression, anxiety, self-criticism, shame, inferiority, and submissive behavior for those patients who practiced compassion-focused processes (Gilbert and Procter 2006).

Compassion as a Form of Validation

It is very important for everyone, but especially children, to have their feelings and experiences validated by others. Lack of validation can result in the development of feelings of guilt and shame in reaction to negative experiences. As a child who was neglected or abused, it is highly likely you didn't receive validation: the abuse itself was very possibly not acknowledged, nor the feelings you experienced because of the abuse. In order to heal from the abuse and the shame surrounding it, it's important that you receive validation now, from yourself and others.

Validation is the recognition and acceptance of another person's internal experience as valid. When someone validates another's experience, the message they send is: "Your feelings make sense. Not only do I hear you, but I understand why you feel as you do. You're not bad or wrong or crazy for feeling the way you do."

Instead of receiving validation, most child victims are ignored, rejected, or judged. Instead of being encouraged to express their feelings, most are shamed into silence. Worse, many have their feelings and perceptions invalidated. To *invalidate* means to attack, dismiss, or question the foundation or reality of a person's feelings. This can be done through denying, ridiculing, ignoring, or judging another person's feelings. Regardless of the method, the effect is clear: the invalidated person feels "wrong." Thus it becomes vitally important that their perceptions and their feelings are validated as a condition of healing. Showing compassion for someone can be a form of validation. And having self-compassion, by connecting to your own suffering with love and acceptance, is a way of validating yourself—your feelings, perception, and experience.

Self-compassion will help you give yourself the nurturance, understanding, and validation you so desperately need in order to feel worthy of care. In fact, as Kristin Neff (2011) stated, when people give themselves empathy and support, they learn to trust that help is always at hand: a powerful message that is the inverse of the lonely helplessness of the abused child.

Practicing Self-Compassion to Break the Cycle of Abuse

As you've learned, shame is a feeling deep within us of being exposed and feeling unworthy. It's also the emotion we most often experience when those parts of ourselves we defend against the most—our weaknesses, deficits, and mistakes—are exposed. The more we hide our weaknesses, the deeper our shame, and the more defenses we need to build up. Those who become abusive tend to have the most defenses; they are defending against their own victimization and shame.

Those caught in a victim pattern tend to always blame themselves when something goes wrong. But those with an abusive pattern do the opposite. When something goes wrong in a relationship, they tend to look outward. It is always someone else's fault, never their own. They turn their feelings of shame into blame. And abusive people are seldom able to have compassion for their victims. All they can think about is that someone hurt or disrespected them, and that they are therefore justified in hurting that person back.

Healing an Abuser Mentality

By practicing self-compassion, an abusive person slowly begins to understand why he took on an abusive pattern. He learns to make the all-important connection between the abuse he experienced and his tendency to become abusive. He becomes more able to have compassion for the small neglected or abused child he was and to use that self-compassion to begin nurturing himself in actions and words. Through self-compassion, an abusive person can learn to forgive himself for his abusive behavior and to connect with how badly he truly feels for what he has done to others. As he gradually begins to feel more forgiving and ultimately more loving toward himself, the self-hatred begins to melt away.

Once a person is healed of debilitating shame, she can afford to lower the wall of defensiveness that protects her from further shaming; by doing so, she frees herself to begin to truly connect with and eventually have compassion for others, which in turn will make her far less likely to re-abuse. In addition, once much of her shame has been eliminated, she can afford to face herself much more honestly, including admitting when she's been abusive in the past and catching herself when she starts to become abusive in the present.

As shame-based defensiveness dwindles, those who took an abusive stance can begin to experience true compassion for their victims. They become able to replace the shame they feel over the harm they caused others with compassion for those they hurt. Finally, they learn that compassion and anger cannot coexist. This cements their conviction to never abuse again.

Healing a Victim Mentality

I shared with you earlier the story of Emily, who came into therapy because she felt she had a problem with low self-esteem. She allowed others to walk all over her and had a difficult time asserting herself. But early on in therapy we established that the reason she, like many victims, put up with unacceptable behavior and was unable to defend herself was because she lacked self-compassion. Without self-compassion, people tend to judge themselves harshly when they make a mistake or when they don't meet their own unreasonable expectations or the high expectations of others. They begin to beat themselves up for not being perfect. In some situations, they begin to feel so badly about themselves that they don't believe they deserve to be treated well by others. And without self-compassion they continue to blame themselves for the horrible ways people treat them—after all, they think, they deserve it. Most importantly, without self-compassion they cannot even acknowledge their pain at having been abused in the past. Without this important acknowledgment, there can be no healing.

Whether you're afraid of becoming abusive or have already begun to abuse either others or yourself, afraid of being victimized or have already established a pattern of being a victim, the Compassion Cure program offers you the information, support, and strategies that will not only help you break the cycle of abuse, but change your life. Instead of living a life stuck in the past, constantly reliving the experience of being emotionally, physically, or sexually abused, you will be able to break free from your past and create a future of your own choosing. Instead of your life being a broken record, constantly replaying the same old refrain, you will be free to write your own song.

Part II

The Compassion Cure Program

It isn't easy for those who were abused in childhood to practice self-compassion. Nor is it easy to accept compassion from someone else. There are many reasons for this. First, most victims were not raised in an environment where compassion was present, much less where it was practiced. Compassion may have been in such short supply that you may have never experienced it from anyone. Second, most people who experienced abuse in childhood haven't been conditioned to be self-compassionate. In fact, you were probably conditioned to be the opposite—self-critical, self-negating, and neglectful of your needs. And third, there are real obstacles in the way of victims being able to accept the concept of compassion. In fact, most victims of abuse have a great deal of resistance to the very idea of self-compassion. For all of these reasons, we'll spend the next few chapters addressing obstacles and resistance to both practicing self-compassion and receiving it from others.

Self-compassion is both a process and a practice. You don't suddenly become self-compassionate. And you can't just decide to become self-compassionate. It will take time and practice to begin viewing yourself in a self-compassionate way and then to begin practicing self-compassion on a daily basis. There is no need to push yourself to become self-compassionate if you aren't ready. In these chapters we'll also focus on some preliminary steps you can take to better prepare yourself to begin the practice of self-compassion. We'll lay the groundwork for a self-compassion practice by introducing ways of thinking and actions that are compatible with self-compassion. For example, you may need to know what receiving compassion from others feels like before you can practice it with yourself.

Finally, I'll teach you mindfulness techniques that will help you cope with and process painful feelings that will inevitably come up as you continue to face the truth about how you were abused and about who abused you. By the time you have completed this section you will be more willing and able to begin your self-compassion practice, which is covered in the third section of the book.

4

The Obstacles to
Self-Compassion

When we are sure that we are on the right road there is no need
to plan our journey too far ahead. No need to burden ourselves
with doubts and fears as to the obstacles that may bar our
progress. We cannot take more than one step at a time.

—Orison Swett Marden

It is completely understandable that those who were abused or
neglected in childhood will have some resistance to the concept and
practice of self-compassion, since many were not treated very compassionately by those around them when they were growing up, and
because shame can make former victims feel so badly about themselves that they don't believe they deserve self-compassion. In this
chapter we will address the various obstacles that former victims face
when contemplating practicing self-compassion. And since we can't
very well have compassion for our suffering if we aren't clear how we
have suffered, we'll also focus on helping you come to a fuller understanding of how you were abused or neglected and how it affected
you.

The Belief That Self-Compassion
Is Self-Indulgent

The most common obstacle to learning and practicing self-
compassion is that many former victims view self-kindness, an

important aspect of self-compassion, as being soft or self-indulgent. This is a common belief in our culture at this particular time, and it's especially harmful when taken on by victims of abuse and neglect, who need self-compassion to heal.

Many of those who were abused in childhood also have a strong belief that to stop and acknowledge their pain and suffering is to "feel sorry for themselves" or "have a pity party." Our culture discourages people from acknowledging and/or talking about their suffering. It's seen as a sign of weakness; and we can even feel embarrassed when we feel bad. It's as if we've done something wrong—as if our personality or our character has failed us in some way. We are supposed to "get over" adversity and "move on," and many people don't have much tolerance or patience for those who don't.

This instant recovery is an extremely unnatural and unreasonable expectation. It takes time to recover from adversity, and healing can't really take place until there is a complete acknowledgment of what actually transpired and how it made the victim feel. So we have a lot of people walking around pretending they weren't adversely affected by a crisis. And God forbid they become identified as "victims"—which has become something of a dirty word in our culture, where victims are shamed and blamed.

People who deny or minimize their own suffering discover that all this pretending and "moving on" will eventually catch up with them in the form of health consequences, many of them stress related. Another negative consequence is that, ironically, the same people who smother and deny their own suffering become intolerant of the pain and suffering of others. The thinking goes like this: "If I got over it, so should you." Their compassion for other people is stunted because they haven't accepted that they themselves need and deserve compassion.

Stopping to acknowledge your suffering with self-compassion is not the same as whining, experiencing self-pity, or feeling sorry for yourself. When we are experiencing self-pity we tend to complain to ourselves about how bad a situation is and see ourselves as helpless to change it. There is often a bitter tone to our thoughts and feelings. While being angry about our situation or about what someone did to hurt us is fine, and even healing, it is when we start to dwell on how we've been victimized, in bitterness and helplessness, that we get stuck in self-pity.

Self-compassion comes from a more nurturing place inside us and can be comforting and validating. Notice the differences between the two statements made by my client Amy, one self-pitying and one self-compassionate:

Self-pity: "No one likes me. I don't have any close friends and I don't have a man in my life. I'm going to be alone for the rest of my life."

Self-compassion: "It's sad I don't have any close friends and I don't have a man in my life right now. I'm afraid I won't ever be loved by a man, and given my history, it's understandable I would have that fear."

This is what Amy noticed: "When I was feeling self-pity I felt bitter. And I felt like, 'poor me.' I also felt hopeless and started to spiral down. But when I practiced being self-compassionate, I noticed I started feeling better after I acknowledged that I felt sad and afraid. And using the phrase 'it is understandable' somehow validated my experience."

Self-compassion can lead to proactive behavior. Once you've validated your feelings and your experience, you may feel more motivated to improve your situation. I often find this to be the case with people who are currently being either emotionally or physically abused. Once they acknowledge their suffering and allow themselves to feel and express their emotions because of it, they often feel more impetus to leave the relationship.

Most of us were raised to just keep going in spite of difficulties. That is all well and good—it's important to persevere—but instead of ignoring our feelings about how difficult something is, it's important to acknowledge the difficulty and have compassion for the fact that we're having it. For example, recovery from abuse can be a long and painful endeavor, and there's a benefit to just putting one foot forward at a time and continuing the journey. But this doesn't mean we don't stop to acknowledge how difficult it can be. In fact, this acknowledgment can give us the motivation to keep going.

The Fear of Becoming Weak, Lazy, or Selfish

Some people worry that if they're compassionate with themselves they're being weak or lacking in a drive to succeed. But if we think about people who are renowned for their compassion, such as Jesus, the Buddha, Gandhi, Florence Nightingale, Mother Teresa, and Nelson Mandela, they can hardly be regarded as weak or unsuccessful. Learning to be self-compassionate can actually make us stronger and more confident.

And some believe that if they give up self-criticism—an important goal of self-compassion—they will become lazy. "It's good for me to be hard on myself," one client told me. "Otherwise, I'll get too lazy and complacent." But in the long run, being hard on yourself doesn't really pay off. No one can be perfect all the time and those who try end up feeling like failures much of the time. It's far more productive to acknowledge how difficult a situation or task is and give yourself encouragement by noticing how far you've come or how well you're doing than to berate yourself because you aren't perfect.

It's also common for people to believe that it's selfish to be self-compassionate. Many of us were taught that we should put others ahead of ourselves; because of this, self-compassion may seem like selfishness. But self-compassion is more than just being nice to yourself or rewarding yourself.

Some people feel guilty when they focus on their suffering. They compare themselves with others who seem to have it worse than they do and they feel they don't have a right to complain. But there will always be someone who has it worse than you, and that doesn't mean you shouldn't take the time to acknowledge your own suffering. Comparing your problems with those of others can also be a convenient way to deny and avoid your own pain, to the benefit of no one.

I told part of Emily's story in chapter 1. She was the woman whose mother was so hard on her, and who knocked her down, kicked her, and locked her out of the house the one time she got enough courage to stand up to her. From Emily's perspective, her mother had it so much worse than she did that she didn't feel she had a right to complain. And she couldn't allow herself to feel her pain about her own suffering or her anger toward her mother. When I asked her if she could have some compassion for her own situation as a child, she responded, "My mother had a horrible life—I had it easy compared to her. She was born in Russia and lived in terrible poverty. Her father left her and her mother when she was five, and her mother had to work long hours in a factory to put food on the table.

"I never wanted for anything. I always had nice clothes and plenty of good food and a beautiful home to live in. Sure my mother went to extremes when it came to insisting that the house was immaculate, but it was because she lived in squalor growing up. She married a man when she was only fifteen because her mother was too sick to work and he promised to take care of her and her mother. But he ended up beating her and putting her to work as a prostitute. She escaped from him and married my father, an American, thirty years older than her. He was one of those men who go to Russia looking for a bride they can control.

"When I think of what my mother went through, I understand why she was the way she was with me. Everything she did, she did so my life would be better than hers. She wanted me to get a good education so I could always support myself and never have to depend on anyone—that's why she insisted I get good grades."

It was good that Emily felt compassion for her mother's suffering. Some victims put up such walls to prevent themselves from being further shamed that they can't feel compassion for anyone. But Emily's compassion for her mother was preventing her from feeling compassion for herself—and from recognizing the connection between her mother's abuse and her current problems.

"Do you remember telling me you ran away from home one time because your mother had beaten you so badly? That you hid in the basement for two days while the police looked for you?" I asked her, hoping I could help her face the truth about how bad it really was for her.

"Yeah, I remember. And there was quite a stink about it, too. It got all over town. My mother was horribly humiliated. I feel bad even today that I put her through that."

"But what about you? It must have been really bad for you to run away. And it must have been horrible for you to be in that cold basement all alone with nothing to eat, afraid of being found by your mother and probably beaten even more for running away."

"Yeah, I was scared, but nothing like my mother must have felt. She didn't know what happened to me or if I was even alive. I put her through hell, and yes, there was hell to pay when she found me, but I deserved it."

It was clear that Emily identified with her mother's suffering so much that she simply could not recognize her own. And she had been blamed so much by her mother for making her life difficult that she continued to blame herself for her own abuse. It was going to take a lot of work on both our parts to help Emily begin to feel compassion for herself.

The Belief That You Are to Blame

As we've discussed, believing you are to blame for the abuse can give you a sense of control, however illusory, over the abuse. If you believe it happened because of something you did or didn't do, then you don't have to face the reality that you were a helpless victim.

Remember, since shame is so debilitating, it makes sense we would do almost anything possible to try to avoid it. Human beings strive to stay in control, both because a sense of control makes us feel safer and because in our society we are raised to believe that we are responsible for what happens to us and that we both can and should control our own lives. Thus, when something goes wrong, we tend to feel ashamed about the fact that we have lost control of our lives. Being victimized causes us to feel helpless, and this helplessness leads us to feel humiliated and ashamed. As a protection against feeling this helplessness and shame, we may take personal responsibility for our own victimization.

It doesn't help that a victim-blaming mentality runs rampant in our culture today. There are even those whose spiritual beliefs hold that if something bad happens to you it is because of your own negative thoughts or attitudes. Cultural influences like this serve to segregate and blame victims rather than encouraging a self-compassionate acknowledgment of suffering.

A Refusal to Acknowledge Your Own Suffering

We can't be moved by our pain if we don't even acknowledge it exists. Denial is a very powerful and effective defense mechanism. Without denial we simply would not survive in some situations. For example, some children are so severely abused or neglected that if they admitted to themselves what their parents did to them, they might commit suicide. In other situations, if a child allowed herself to acknowledge how much she was suffering at the hands of her abuser, she might not be able to stay sane.

Denial can certainly be your friend, keeping you alive in unbearable situations; but at this point, it may have become your enemy. You may have survived the actual abuse, but unless you face the truth about what happened to you and why it happened, you will not be able to fully heal. Unless you stop blaming yourself for the abuse and face the pain of admitting that someone you cared about could treat you in such damaging, selfish, callous ways, you are likely to continue to punish yourself in the form of self-destructive behaviors or to repeat the cycle of abuse, either getting involved with people who abuse you or becoming abusive yourself.

Those who were abused in childhood are often so good at making excuses for their abusers, minimizing how hurt and damaged they were by the abuse, or denying that abuse even took place that they need help taking such blinders off and allowing their suffering to surface. The following exercise can help.

Exercise: Your Childhood from a Different Perspective

Write the story of your childhood as though you were writing about someone else entirely, and you are simply a storyteller ("There was once a little girl who had a mean stepfather..."). The child is the subject of the story, so as you write, give details of what happened and what the child did, thought, and felt. Keep the perspective of the storyteller who knows what happened to and around the child and how the child experienced the events, but who is separate from the action.

This technique can help you view your childhood from a different perspective entirely. In fact, it has helped some victims recognize their suffering for the very first time. This happened with Emily.

I asked Emily to write about her childhood from a storyteller's perspective. I emphasized that this was her story, not her mother's; I believe this helped her stop comparing her suffering with her mother's. This is what she came up with.

"There was once a little girl who lived in a beautiful house with her mother. Because there was no father in the home and her mother worked, the little girl had the responsibility of keeping the house clean and the yard maintained. This was a lot for the girl to do, but she did her best. Sometimes she was so tired she couldn't stay awake at school and so she sometimes didn't do as well in school as she might have. This made her mother really angry, and she would yell at the girl and call her names. This made the girl feel very bad. She wanted to do well in school but she was just too tired sometimes. She didn't know what to do. She felt like a failure and a disappointment to her mother. This made the little girl feel depressed, so depressed that sometimes she thought about running away and in fact, this is what she did one time. But this only made her mother worry and made the little girl feel even worse about herself. So she thought about killing herself. That way she wouldn't continue to disappoint her mother."

When Emily wrote about her childhood from this perspective it really opened her eyes. She told me she had forgotten about thinking about suicide and about just how terrible she felt about herself. And when she read the piece aloud to me, she broke down crying, telling me she hadn't realized just how difficult it had been growing up with her mother's demands. She said she felt sorry for the girl in the story and recognized that her mother's expectations of her had been unreasonable. This was a breakthrough in Emily's therapy. Finally, she was able to acknowledge her own suffering and have real compassion for herself.

Not Understanding How You Suffered

Another primary reason why those who were abused in childhood resist acknowledging their suffering is that they simply don't understand *how* they have suffered. Either they don't know about all the ways in which they were abused or they don't understand how the abuse has affected them. They may simply be uneducated about what constitutes childhood neglect and abuse, or they may refuse to believe that the treatment they endured was actually abuse.

In this section I will name and describe the various types of emotional, physical, and sexual abuse experienced by children. My hope is that these lists and descriptions will help you in two ways: (1) that they'll help you get past any vestiges of denial you may have about the fact that you were, indeed, abused; and (2) that they'll help you identify ways you've been abused that you may not currently be aware of.

Many victims will have clear memories of being abused or neglected as children. But some people's memories are not so clear, and some question the memories they do have. Others haven't labeled their experiences as abuse or neglect even though that is clearly what they experienced. So I've provided a brief overview of exactly what constitutes childhood abuse and neglect. All these forms of abuse can occur separately, but they often occur in combination; for example, emotional abuse is almost always a part of physical abuse.

A word of warning: this overview of the various types of abuse may be triggering for you. If you don't feel you are strong enough at this time to read through a comprehensive and detailed list of types of child abuse and neglect, please give yourself permission to skip this. You can always return to it at a later time. (If you do choose to skip this section, you can go directly to "Releasing Your Anger," later in this chapter.)

Neglect

Neglect of a child is when a caretaker fails to provide for the child's basic physical needs as well as her emotional, social, educational, and medical needs. Physical needs include providing adequate food, water, shelter, and attention to personal hygiene. It also involves providing adequate supervision. (Leaving a very young child alone at home while the parent is at work or otherwise away, or leaving him in the care of someone who is not fit to care for him, therefore qualifies as neglect of those needs.) Emotional needs include emotional security and encouragement. Social needs include providing opportunities for the child to interact with other children of an appropriate age. Educational needs include providing the child with experiences necessary for growth and development, such as sending the child to school and attending to special educational needs. Medical needs include basic health care, as well as dental care and mental health treatments. (Please note that failure to provide for these needs only applies when options are available to caretakers.)

Emotional Abuse

Emotional abuse is any nonphysical behavior or attitude that serves to control, intimidate, subjugate, demean, punish, or isolate another person. Emotional abuse of a child includes acts or omissions by parents or caretakers that can cause serious behavioral, cognitive, emotional, or mental disorders in the child. This form of maltreatment includes verbal abuse (constant criticism, belittling, insulting, rejecting, and teasing); placing excessive, aggressive, or unreasonable demands on a child, demands beyond her capabilities; and failure to provide the emotional and psychological nurturing and support necessary for a child's emotional and psychological growth and development.

Psychological Maltreatment

While psychological maltreatment is sometimes considered a subset of emotional abuse, this term is often used by professionals to describe a *concerted attack* by an adult on a child's development of self and social competence—a pattern of psychically destructive behavior that is often *more* deliberate and conscious on the parents' or other caregivers' part than typical emotional abuse. Under this definition, psychological maltreatment is classified into the following forms of behavior:

- Rejecting: behaviors that communicate or constitute abandonment of the child, such as a refusal to speak to or acknowledge the child or show affection

- Isolating: preventing the child from participating in normal opportunities for social interaction

- Terrorizing: threatening the child with severe or sinister punishment, or deliberately developing a climate of fear or threat

- Ignoring: being psychologically unavailable to the child and failing to respond to the child's needs or behavior

- Corrupting: encouraging the child to develop false social values that reinforce antisocial or deviant behavioral patterns, such as aggression, criminality, or substance abuse

- Withholding: deliberately withholding attention, love, support, or guidance

- ❀ Degrading: acts or behaviors that degrade or humiliate children, such as making fun of their physical appearance in front of others

- ❀ Stimulus deprivation: refusing to provide activities and experiences that children need for growth and education

- ❀ Negative influence: exposing the child to unhealthy role models (drug addicts, prostitutes, criminals)

- ❀ Forcing children to live in dangerous and unstable environments (for example, exposure to domestic violence or parental conflict)

Physical Abuse

The physical abuse of a child (anyone under the age of eighteen) includes any non-accidental physical injury or pattern of injuries. This may include:

- ❀ Slapping or punching a child so hard that it causes marks or bruises

- ❀ Kicking a child using such force that it knocks the child down or causes marks or bruises

- ❀ Beating a child with an object

- ❀ Burning a child with a cigarette, putting a child's hand in the fire, and so on

- ❀ Biting a child

- ❀ Twisting a child's arm to the point that it causes bruising or fractures

- ❀ Shaking a child so hard it causes dizziness, disorientation, headaches, or neck, shoulder, or arm pain

- ❀ Holding a child's head under water

- ✿ Shoving a child against a wall, across the room, or into furniture

- ✿ Pinning a child down on the floor and not letting her get up

- ✿ Pinching a child so hard it causes severe pain and/or bruising

Sexual Abuse

Child sexual abuse includes any contact between an adult and a child, or between an older child and a younger child, that is for the purposes of sexual stimulation of the child or the adult or older child, and that results in sexual gratification *for the older person*. This can range from nontouching offenses, such as exhibitionism or showing the child pornography, to fondling, penetration, creating child pornography, and child prostitution. A child doesn't have to be touched to be sexually molested.

It's generally agreed that an "older child" is two or more years older than the younger child, but an age difference of even one year can have tremendous power implications—enough to make a situation abusive. For example, an older sibling is almost always seen as an authority figure, especially if he is left "in charge" when the parents are away. His sister may go along with his demands out of fear or out of a need to please. In cases of sibling incest, the greater the age difference, the greater the betrayal of trust, and the more violent the incest tends to be.

Child sexual abuse can include any of the following:

- ✿ Genital exposure: the adult or older child exposes his or her genitals to the child.

- ✿ Kissing: the adult or older child kisses the child in a lingering or intimate way.

- ✿ Fondling: the adult or older child fondles the child's breasts, abdomen, genital area, inner thighs, or buttocks. The child may also be asked to touch the older person's body in these places.

⚜ Masturbation: the adult or older child masturbates while the child observes; the adult observes the child masturbating; the adult and child masturbate each other (mutual masturbation).

⚜ Fellatio: the adult or older child has the child fellate him or her, or the adult fellates the child.

⚜ Cunnilingus: either the child is coerced or made to place his mouth and tongue in the vaginal area of an adult female or older female child, or the adult places his mouth in the vaginal area of the female child.

⚜ Digital penetration: the adult or older child inserts a finger or fingers into the vagina or anus of the child. Perpetrators may also thrust inanimate objects such as crayons or pencils inside.

⚜ Penile penetration: the adult or older child penetrates the child's vagina or anus with his penis.

⚜ Frottage: the adult or older child rubs his genitals or other body parts against the child's genital-rectal area or inner thighs or buttocks.

⚜ Pornography: the adult or older child shows the child pornographic materials, usually for the purpose of priming the child for sexual contact or sexually stimulating the child.

Subtle or Hidden Forms of Emotional, Physical, and Sexual Abuse

Most people reading this book already know they were abused in childhood and that they suffer from shame because of it. But in addition to the abuse you have already identified, you may have also been abused in other, less obvious ways. Below is a description of some lesser known, more hidden forms of abuse, which can be just as shaming as the more overt forms of abuse.

Subtle Forms of Emotional Abuse

In parent/child relationships, subtle forms of emotional abuse can take many forms, including:

- Ignoring, or withholding of attention or affection, including "the silent treatment"

- Disapproving, dismissive, contemptuous, or condescending looks, comments, and behavior

- Subtle threats of abandonment (either physical or emotional)

- Invalidation (not acknowledging the child's feelings or experience)

- Making a child feel in the way or unwanted

- Blaming a child for his parent's problems or circumstances

- Projecting the parent's own problems or issues onto a child

- Encouraging a child to be overly dependent on the parent

- Causing a child to feel inadequate or incapable of taking care of herself

Sometimes parents deliberately shame their children into minding without realizing the disruptive impact shame can have on the child's sense of self. Statements such as "You should be ashamed of yourself" or "Shame on you" are obvious examples. Yet because these kinds of statements are overtly shaming, they are actually easier for the child to defend against than more subtle forms of shaming such as contempt, humiliation, and public shaming. For example, behavior that has been acceptable at home is suddenly seen by parents as bad in public. Or the parent seems to be ashamed because his child is not adhering to social norms that the child was completely unaware of. Such comments as "Stop that, you're embarrassing me in front of everyone" not only cause a child to feel exposed, judged, and ashamed, but burden him with his parent's shame as well.

There are many ways that parents shame their children. These include:

Belittling. Comments such as "You're too old to want to be held" or "You're just a crybaby" are horribly humiliating to a child. When a parent makes a negative comparison between his child and another ("Why can't you act like Tommy? Tommy isn't a crybaby"), it is not only humiliating, but it teaches a child to always compare himself with peers and find himself deficient in the comparison.

Blaming. When a child makes a mistake, such as accidentally hitting a ball through a neighbor's window, he needs to take responsibility. But many parents go way beyond teaching the child a lesson, instead blaming and berating the child: "You stupid idiot! You should have known better than to play so close to the house! Now I'm going to have to pay for that window. I don't have enough money to constantly be cleaning up your messes!" All this accomplishes is to shame the child so much that he cannot find a way to walk away from the situation with his head held high. Blaming the child like this is like rubbing his nose in the mess he made, and it produces such intolerable shame that he may be forced to deny responsibility or find ways of excusing it.

Contempt. Expressions of disgust or contempt communicate absolute rejection. The look of contempt (often a sneer or curled lip), especially from someone who is significant to a child, can be a devastating inducer of shame, because the child is made to feel disgusting or offensive. When I was a child my mother had an extremely negative attitude toward me. Much of the time she looked at me with either an expectant look that said, "What are you up to now?" or one of disapproval or disgust over what I had already done. These looks were extremely shaming to me, causing me to feel that there was something terribly wrong with me.

Humiliation. As Gershen Kaufman stated in his book *Shame: The Power of Caring* (1992): "There is no more humiliating experience than to have another person who is clearly the stronger and more powerful take advantage of that power and give us a beating." I can attest to this. In addition to shaming me with her contemptuous looks, my mother often punished me by hitting me with the limb off a tree, and she often did this outside, in front of the neighbors. The humiliation I felt was like a deep wound to my soul.

Disabling Expectations. Appropriate parental expectations serve as necessary guides to behavior and are not disabling. Disabling expectations, on the other hand, have to do with pressuring a child to excel at a task, skill, or activity. Parents who have an inordinate need for their child to excel at a particular activity or skill are likely to behave in ways that pressure the child to do more and more. According to Kaufman, when a child becomes aware of the real possibility of failing to meet parental expectations, he often experiences a binding self-consciousness. This self-consciousness—the painful watching of oneself—is very disabling. When something is expected of us in this way, attaining the goal is made harder, if not impossible (Kaufman 1992).

Parents induce shame in their children by communicating to them that they are a disappointment. Such messages as "I can't believe you could do such a thing" or "I am deeply disappointed in you" accompanied by a disapproving tone of voice and facial expression can crush a child's spirit. These messages are a form of disabling expectations.

Subtle Forms of Physical Abuse

Although emotional abuse usually includes only nonphysical forms of abuse, it can include what is called *symbolic violence,* which can be a subtle form of physical abuse. This includes intimidating behavior such as slamming doors; kicking a wall; throwing dishes, furniture, or other objects; driving recklessly while the victim is in the car; and destroying or threatening to destroy objects the victim values. Even milder forms of violence, such as shaking a fist or finger at the victim, making threatening gestures or faces, or the abuser acting like she wants to hurt or kill the victim, carry symbolic threats of violence.

Such subtle physical abuse by a parent of a child can also include keeping a strap, belt, or paddle on display for the child to see, and pointing at the strap whenever the child doesn't instantly do as the parent says; or standing over a child in an intimidating way to get him to do something.

Subtle Forms of Child Sexual Abuse

Subtle forms of sexual abuse can include any of the following. Keep in mind that it is the *intention* of the adult or older child while engaging in these activities that determines whether the act is sexually abusive.

- ❀ Nudity: the adult or older child parades around the house in front of the child without clothes on.

- ❀ Disrobing: the adult or older child disrobes in front of the child, generally when the child and the older person are alone.

- ❀ Observation of the child: the adult or older child surreptitiously or overtly watches the child undress, bathe, excrete, or urinate.

- ❀ Inappropriate comments: the adult or older child makes inappropriate comments about the child's body. This can include making comments about the child's developing body (comments about the size of a boy's penis or of a girl's breasts), or asking a teenager to share intimate details about his dating life.

- ❀ Sexualized touching: even back rubs or tickling can have a sexual aspect to them if the person doing it has a sexual agenda.

- ❀ Emotional incest: a parent romanticizes the relationship between herself and her child, treats the child as if he were her intimate partner, or is seductive with a child. This can also include a parent confiding in a child about his adult sexual relationships and sharing intimate sexual details with a child or adolescent.

❀ Approach behavior: this is any indirect or direct sexual suggestion made by an adult or older child toward a child. This can include sexual looks, innuendos, or suggestive gestures. Even if the older person never engaged in touching or took any overt sexual action, the sexual feelings that are projected are picked up by the child.

These lists can be helpful in further clarifying what constitutes emotional, physical, and sexual child abuse. Although you may be aware of many of the more obvious forms of abuse, you may be surprised to discover that behaviors you thought were normal are actually considered abusive and can cause considerable damage to a child's psyche, in addition to great shame.

Your Reactions to This Information

It's very possible that you have some rather strong reactions to reading the preceding material, including surprise, shame, and anger. You may feel surprised or even shocked at your degree of denial about your abuse experiences. If this is the case, remember that whatever your level of denial, it was once necessary for you to keep going, or even to survive or stay sane. If you can, have compassion for yourself for needing to be in denial, instead of criticizing yourself for something you couldn't help at the time.

It's possible you may feel overwhelmed with anger and disbelief at how many forms of abuse you suffered. This can be the case whether you have fully faced the truth about your abuse, are just coming out of denial, or are somewhere on the path between denial and acknowledgment. It is common for victims to experience a great deal of anger and rage at having been victimized, and you have a right to your anger: it is a natural reaction to being shamed and humiliated. But it probably was not safe for you to express your anger or rage at the time of the abuse—or even to feel it. Releasing your anger now can empower you, and motivate you to continue on your healing journey. The good news is that there are techniques that can help you safely release your anger without the fear of being punished, further shamed, or abused.

Releasing Your Anger

Some healthy, constructive ways to vent your anger around the abuse you suffered include the following. Consider any or all of these, depending on what seems to speak to you about your angry feelings.

- ❁ Write a letter to your abuser that you do not send, letting him or her know exactly how the abuse affected you. Don't hold back: let all your feelings of anger and hurt come out on the page.

- ❁ Walk around your house (assuming you are alone) and talk out loud to yourself, expressing all the angry feelings you are having. Don't censor yourself: say exactly what is on your mind in whatever language you choose.

- ❁ Imagine you are sitting across from your abuser (choose one if there were more than one) and tell him or her exactly how you feel about what he or she did to you. Again, don't hold back and don't censor yourself. If you notice you are afraid to confront your abuser in this way, imagine that your abuser is tied to the chair. If you don't want to see his or her eyes for fear of becoming intimidated, imagine that he or she is blind-folded. And if you are afraid of what he or she might say to you in response to your anger, imagine that he or she is gagged.

- ❁ Put your face in a pillow and scream.

✿ If you feel like you need to release your anger physically, ask your body what it needs to do. You might get the sense that you need to hit, kick, push, break things, or tear things up. Honor that intuitive feeling by finding a way to release your anger in that's safe, but satisfying. For example, it is safe to kneel down next to your bed and hit the mattress with your fists. If you are alone and no one is around you can let out sounds as you hit. You can lie on your bed and kick your legs, or you can stomp on egg cartons or other packaging; you can tear up old telephone books, or go to a deserted place and throw rocks or bottles.

If you have difficulty giving yourself permission to get angry, or have fears of losing control if you get angry, I urge you to refer to my book *Honor Your Anger* (2004). I also write extensively about getting past your resistance to releasing anger in my book *The Right to Innocence: Healing the Trauma of Childhood Sexual Abuse* (1989). Either of these books will help you work past your fears and resistance, and both offer many more suggestions on how to release anger in constructive, safe ways.

Releasing our anger about having been abused has a significant benefit: it helps us recognize that the abuse was not our fault. Although we may know on an *intellectual* level that, as children, we did not cause those who abused us to act as they did, and did not deserve the abuse either, expressing our anger at having been abused helps us know these truths on a much deeper level.

It is especially important for those who *internalized* their anger (blaming themselves) to redirect that anger toward their abuser. After all, the abuser is the appropriate target for that anger. When we allow ourselves to get angry at our abusers, the vital force of anger will be moving in the right direction: outward instead of inward.

Internalizing your anger and blame not only makes you feel guilty and ashamed but can also cause you to punish yourself with negative relationships or self-destructive behavior (such as alcohol or drug abuse, starving yourself, overeating, or self-mutilation). Letting all that self-hatred become righteous anger toward your abuser allows you to stop taking your anger *out on* yourself and start taking it *out of* yourself.

Releasing your anger at the abuser can also help you give the shame back to the abuser—after all, it is his or her shame that was put on you. The following exercise will help you to do this.

Exercise: Giving Back Your Abuser's Shame

1. Ground yourself by placing your feet flat on the floor and taking some deep breaths.

2. Imagine you are able to look inside your body. Scan your body and see if you can locate where the shame surrounding the abuse is located. Find any shame or any feelings that you are "bad" currently present in your body.

3. Imagine you are reaching inside your body and pulling out that dark, ugly stuff.

4. Now imagine you are throwing all that dark ugliness at your abuser, where it belongs. Open your eyes and make a throwing motion with your arms.

5. Say out loud as you do it: "There, take back your shame. It's yours, not mine."

Some clients have reported that when they visualized they found so much shame inside that they had to go back several times in order to get all of it. If you find this to be true for you, just break off, or grab as much shame as you can, throw it away, and then go back for more.

This exercise may bring up more anger or it may bring up sadness. Whatever emotions arise, allow yourself to express them freely, constructively, and safely.

If you feel like confronting your abuser(s) directly, I encourage you to continue releasing your anger in healthy, constructive ways first so that you do not put yourself or the other person at risk. I also encourage you to carefully consider whether it is safe for you (emotionally and physically) to confront your abuser. If the person has not changed, he or she could become physically or emotionally abusive toward you, causing you to be retraumatized. For more information on the pros and cons of direct confrontations, please read my books *Breaking the Cycle of Abuse* (2005) or *The Right to Innocence* (1989).

Coping with Feelings of Numbness or Sadness

Instead of feeling angry, you may feel numb. Your awareness of how you have been abused or to what extent you were abused may be so overwhelming that you've shut down emotionally. If you find you have difficulty discerning just what your emotions are as you revisit the details of what happened to you, please take care of yourself physically and emotionally. Rest, take a warm bath, talk to a close friend, drink a cup of tea, put on a soft sweater, watch a favorite movie, read from a book of meditations—do whatever it is you do to soothe and comfort yourself. If you feel safe enough and strong enough to go outside, taking a long walk can help ground you and bring you back to the present.

In realizing that you were abused in more ways than you realized or in facing the abuse once again, you may feel deeply saddened. If this is true for you, allow yourself to feel this sadness; let the tears flow. If you have resistance to feeling sadness, or fear becoming depressed or not being able to stop crying once you start, chapter 6 will help you work through these concerns. There we'll focus on strategies that will allow you to feel your deep sadness without becoming overwhelmed by it.

When you are ready, please take the time to write about all the types of abuse you experienced.

Exercise: Recognizing the Ways You Were Abused

1. Begin by writing down the facts of each type of abuse you suffered: what, who, when, and where. Use the material in this chapter to guide you as needed, and take your time.

2. When you have finished this document, revisit it. This time, describe how each experience of abuse affected your life, both at the time and as time went by.

This exercise will take some time, and you will probably need to work on it in more than one sitting. When you are done, set it aside; we will use it in later chapters.

There may be many obstacles in the way of your feeling and practicing self-compassion, including denial of the extent and nature of your suffering, shame, self-blame, and overwhelming emotions surrounding the abuse. But you don't have to allow these obstacles to keep you from experiencing the healing power of compassion. By acknowledging that the treatment you experienced was not normal but was actually abusive, by not blaming yourself for the abuse, and by continuing to come out of denial about how the abuse you suffered negatively affected you, you can learn to have compassion for yourself and heal your shame.

There is one more obstacle to practicing self-compassion that many victims encounter: they may have an extremely difficult time feeling compassion for themselves because they never experienced it from anyone else. They never had a safe environment in which kindness and support were offered. The next chapter explores the details of this obstacle, and offers the experience of receiving compassion to those who have not yet been able to experience this healing emotional exchange.

5 Receiving Compassion from Others

If you find a path with no obstacles, it
probably doesn't lead anywhere.

—Frank A. Clark

In the previous chapter, we discussed the obstacles to practicing self-compassion—denial, self-blame, shame, and others. Here, we'll focus on common obstacles to receiving compassion (there are some similarities), and on how to overcome these. And if you have been missing the experience of receiving compassion from others—a necessary experience if one is to practice self-compassion—you will have the opportunity to experience it here.

Obstacles to Taking in Compassion

Many victims of abuse refuse to take in compassion from others because they believe they don't need or deserve it, or it simply doesn't apply to them. For example, often when I attempt to offer compassion to a new client for how she has suffered due to abuse, she tries to play it down by saying something like "The abuse really hasn't caused that many problems in my life" or "The past is the past. I've gotten over it." This is always interesting to hear, since the person began therapy with me because something wasn't working in her life.

If you can relate to these statements, it may be an indication that you are still in some degree of denial about how much the abuse negatively affected you. Even if you are now aware of how much shame is currently affecting your life, you may find that you sink back into denial from time to time and take on the attitude exemplified above. The following exercise may help you to look a little deeper at your denial and understand why it is still such a powerful force in your life.

Exercise: Exploring Your Denial

1. I'm afraid to admit I was abused in this way because _____ .

2. If I admit I was abused, I will have to feel _____ .

3. If I admit how much the abuse has affected me _____ .

4. I don't want to face the truth about my abuser because _____ .

5. I'm afraid to allow myself to feel my anger (or sadness) because _____ .

Living in a Culture of Denial

Our culture frowns upon people acknowledging their suffering. In fact, it celebrates people who have "overcome" adversity and "moved on." Time after time we see victims of natural disasters such as floods, forest fires, and tornados interviewed on television. Reporters ask the victims, "How are you feeling?" and many smile for the cameras and say something like "I'm just glad to be alive. We will rebuild" or "It's just material things." This is what viewers want to hear. They don't want to hear, "I'm devastated. I've lost everything. I don't know if I can go on," which is what many victims in these situations actually feel. It has become so commonplace for us to put on a happy face that it can be shocking to hear when someone is honest about how much they are suffering.

If you are surrounded by people who believe you should just "get over it," please realize you have a right to your feelings and a right to do whatever you can to help yourself recover from the abuse, including reaching out to those who can provide you with the compassion you need and learning how to provide self-compassion for yourself.

Feeling Undeserving of Compassion

Many people who experienced child abuse are so full of shame that they believe they don't deserve compassion or kindness from others. If you firmly believe you are a "bad person," as many victims do, the compassion of others may not only feel undeserved but may even make you feel angry or impatient.

This is how my client Kyle responded when I offered compassion for what he suffered as a child: "Don't feel sorry for me. You don't understand. I was really a bad kid. I was always in trouble at school. In fact, I was one of those kids who bullied other kids. I would look for a weak kid and then I got off on making his life miserable.

"When I got older I started shoplifting. I justified it because we were so poor. I got caught and they told me that if I went into that store again they'd put me in juvenile hall. My dad nearly killed me for that one, but it didn't do any good. By the time I got to high school I had graduated to stealing cars."

"So what do you think made you so bad?" I inquired.

"I don't know—born that way, I guess."

"Like a bad seed?"

"Yeah, something like that. My poor mother. I think I was just too much for her. She 'took to bed' by the time I was ten or so. That's what they called it back then. She was always in bed but I was never clear what the problem was. She seemed healthy enough…I think she just gave up trying to be a mother. It was too much for her."

"So she didn't discipline you when you got into trouble?"

"No, that was my dad's job. He really let us have it when we messed up."

"What did he do?"

"He hit us with his belt—and he didn't hold back! You wouldn't believe how much it hurt—especially when the buckle hit you. Man..."

"So did that make you stop being bad?"

"No, it made me angrier. I just went away in my head. I'd think about what I'd like to do to him. And I never cried. I wasn't going to give him the satisfaction..."

"Do you think your dad was wrong—do you think he was abusive?"

"Don't make me out to be a victim! He was old school. His dad was just like him. You know, spare the rod and spoil the child."

"What's your relationship with him like today?"

"I'm not close to either of my parents. I left home and never looked back."

Kyle was so full of shame from his father's abuse and his mother's neglect that he was convinced he was a bad person. It was going to take a lot of work on both our parts to help him recognize that he had good reasons for his bad behavior. We'll follow Kyle's progress later in the book.

Having Difficulty Taking In the Good

Another reason why victims of abuse don't feel they deserve compassion from others is that they have a difficult time taking in anything good—whether it be compliments, acknowledgments, gifts, success, even love. This is another consequence of having been shamed by abuse. If you feel overwhelmed with shame, you don't believe you deserve good things that come your way, and so you push them away somehow.

Do you have a difficult time accepting compliments? Do you say things like "Oh, this old thing, I've had it for years" when someone compliments what you are wearing? Do you respond with "Oh, thanks, but I think I look tired" when someone compliments you on how you look?

Is receiving gifts also difficult for you? Some people quickly thank the person and then just put the gift aside, not really taking the time to look at it carefully. Many of my clients confess that they usually put gifts in a closet or drawer and don't ever use them, or they give them to someone else. Others report they have a tendency to be critical of gifts they receive—always finding something wrong with them. Still others avoid having to acknowledge a gift by assuming that the other person put no thought into it or by assuming the person re-gifted. In this way they don't have to take in the possibility that the other person actually cared about them enough to pick out something special for them.

Taking in a compliment or a gift can make you feel uncomfortable if you don't feel good about yourself and don't think you deserve good things. The same goes for taking in compassion given to you by someone else. But you can learn to take in good things. The next time you receive a compliment, try the following exercise.

Exercise: Learning to Take a Compliment

1. Don't say anything right away.

2. Instead, take a deep breath and imagine that you are taking the compliment inside you with the breath.

3. Notice how that feels. If you notice that it feels uncomfortable, try to allow that feeling without judging it (strategies for how to do this will be given in the next chapter).

4. Breathe out, look the person in the eye, and say, "Thank you." If you are moved to add something positive or neutral, like "It's my favorite shirt," do so. If you are moved to say something more negative like "This is so old, I'm surprised you like it," take note of that urge but resist it. "Thank you," with a moment of eye contact and perhaps a smile, is all you need.

5. It can be helpful to take time to reflect on your experience with this exercise (for example, how uncomfortable it was to take in the compliment) and to write about any feelings that came up or any memories or associations you made.

95

You can do the same thing when you receive a gift. Before you say anything, take a deep breath and consciously take in the fact that this person took the time to choose a gift for you. If you tend to push gifts away with critical thoughts, try not to let your mind run amok. Instead, tell yourself, "Just take it in" or "Just appreciate the gesture." Later, you can reflect on and write about any uncomfortable feelings that might have come up and any memories you may have around gift-giving (never getting what you asked for as a kid; being shamed for not showing enough gratitude).

The belief that you do not deserve good things is a very powerful one, so you will need to go through this process many times before you become more comfortable taking in compliments or receiving gifts. Eventually, though, you will notice that taking in a deep breath, and with it the positive feeling of being cared about, will begin to feel good, and you will have little or no need to push away the good things that come your way.

Once you have learned how to take in compliments and gifts, you will be in a better position to take in compassion from others. Just follow the same process of breathing deeply and allowing yourself to take in and feel the compassion that is being offered.

Keeping Up Our Emotional Walls

Still another reason why some have difficulty taking in compassion from others is that it makes them feel too vulnerable. This was part of the reason Kyle resisted taking in compassion from me. Because he was shamed so severely by his father, Kyle had built up an emotional wall to protect himself from being further shamed. Now this wall was in the way of his allowing himself to feel vulnerable. For Kyle, feeling vulnerable was equivalent to being weak, and for him, being weak meant he wouldn't survive. To take in the compassion I was offering, he would have to lower that wall and be vulnerable, and this felt dangerous to him.

If you have built up a defensive wall in order to protect yourself from experiencing more shame, it may be difficult for you to lower that wall, even to take in compassion, kindness, or love from someone else. Kindness and compassion can cause unresolved feelings of sadness and grief to be ignited. Some people become overwhelmed by the pain of their grief or even dissociate from it (that is, disconnect from their body). Others are afraid that if they take in the kindness and compassion of others, it will be taken away or they will have to pay for it later.

As you allow yourself to take in compassion, you may find that feelings of sadness or anger come up. As much as you can, just allow yourself to feel these emotions. Sadness may come up if, in that moment, you become keenly aware that you have not received compassion in the past. And receiving compassion from someone may feel like permission to feel all the pain that you have never allowed yourself to feel. The same thing can occur with anger: once you receive validation and comfort in the form of compassion, you may suddenly feel the anger that you never allowed yourself to feel before. In the next chapter we'll explore ways to process these feelings of sadness and anger and not become overwhelmed by them.

Receiving the Compassion You Missed Out On

In the remainder of this chapter I will offer you the kind of safe environment, kindness, and support that you may have missed out on growing up. I will do this in three ways: by offering compassionate statements directly to you; by asking you to think of the kinds of compassionate words you wish you had heard when you were a child; and by encouraging you to actively look for people and environments where you can share your story and your suffering and be reasonably certain you will receive compassion in return.

To get the benefit of the exercises and opportunities for reflection in the rest of this chapter, please prepare by doing the following:

⚘ Have the list you created at the end of chapter 4, of all the ways you were abused as a child, handy.

⊛   Choose a time and a place conducive to this kind of work; for example, a private place where you are alone, with all electronics turned off.

⊛   When you do the exercises, sit quietly with your feet on the ground. Take a few deep breaths, try to clear your mind, and relax your body as much as you can.

It would be ideal if you could devote several hours of quiet time, in one block, to reading this material and completing the exercises, but it's perfectly fine to work on one part at a time, completing one a day or even one a week. Take at least half an hour to work through each part.

Part 1: Taking In Words of Compassion

The exercise below (and the variation that follows a bit later) is designed to help you have the experience of hearing words of compassion from someone else. Please do the best you can to be open to the experience, even if you find it difficult.

Exercise: Imagine I Am with You

1. Imagine if you can that I, Beverly, am sitting with you wherever you are.

2. Now bring out the list you made at the end of chapter 4 of all the ways you were abused in childhood.

3. Slowly read your list to yourself in silence. Notice how you feel as you read your list.

4. Now read your list once again, this time out loud. Imagine you are talking directly to me. Again, notice how you feel.

5. Once you have read your list out loud, please read the following passage silently to yourself. Try to imagine I am saying these words, talking directly to you:

"I want you to know how sorry I am that you have suffered so much and so deeply because of the abuse you have experienced. No one should have to suffer the way you have. I know you have felt alone with your suffering, thinking that no one could possibly understand and that no one really cares. But I want you to know I do understand your suffering and I do care.

"I understand because I too am an abuse survivor. But I also understand because in the years I have been in practice I have heard thousands of clients tell me about their abuse experiences, and this has given me a deep understanding of how abuse can cause people to suffer. I care because I don't believe anyone should have to suffer alone and because I believe that knowing that someone cares makes any suffering a little more tolerable."

Please sit quietly for a few minutes and try to take in my words. If you are having difficulty, follow my instructions from earlier in the chapter about how to learn to take in good things. Read the words again, take a deep breath, and take the words inside you.

My words of compassion in the preceding exercise may or may not have had an effect on you. While you may believe I understand what you have been through, it may also be difficult to believe that I could actually care about *you*. After all, I don't know you or your individual story. And even if I were actually in your presence, as your therapist, it might be difficult to believe that a stranger could really care about you. I've had many clients tell me in the beginning of counseling that they can't believe I care—I am being paid for the sessions and that's why I am listening. But I promise you, I do care. My motivation for this work has never been about money. I deliberately charge rates that are low so that victims of abuse can afford my services. And the many hours I spend writing my books could never be recompensed. I do this work because it is my mission in life. It feels right for me to pass on the knowledge, the wisdom, and the compassion that I have been so fortunate to receive.

Most of my clients through the years, even those who have the most difficult time trusting and believing someone could care about them, come to a place where they believe I genuinely care about them. My hope is that by continuing to read this book and staying open to learning who I am through reading these pages, you too will come to feel my genuine caring for you.

If you find you have a difficult time taking in my words of understanding and caring, try the exercise again, this time imagining you are reading your list to someone you feel understands you and cares about you. If you have no one in your life who fits this description, think of a person you have seen or met but don't know well (you could choose a fictional character) who appears to be understanding and caring. Imagine this person is sitting quietly with you as you read aloud, and then that this person says to you the kind words offered above. Notice whether you're able to take the words in any more easily with this understanding person saying them.

If you were able to take these words in—either by imagining I am saying them to you or that another loving, compassionate person is—you may wish to return to them often, either reading them silently to yourself or out loud.

Part 2: Taking In the Words You Wish You Had Heard

When you were being abused you felt painfully alone. There was no one there to save or comfort you. But the time right after the abuse may have been even more difficult. You may have dissociated while being abused, and once the abuse ended you may have come crashing back to reality. And once the abuser was no longer in your presence, you may have felt even more alone. Hearing the words of comfort that you needed after you were abused, even now, perhaps years after the fact, can be healing.

Using the document you created in chapter 4 to reflect on each of the types of abuse you suffered, spend a few minutes with the following exercise, thinking about what you wish you had heard from someone right after you were abused.

Exercise: What Do You Wish You Had Heard?

1. Write down the words of comfort you so desperately needed to hear from someone.

2. Read the words out loud and imagine that someone you cared about had actually spoken these words to you at the time.

3. Take a deep breath and really let the words in. Notice how you feel when you hear these words. Allow yourself to cry if you feel like it.

4. Write these statements on an index card and place it somewhere where you can readily see them. Or copy them into your journal so you can read them to yourself again and again.

This can be a very powerful experience. In addition to imagining the words you wished you had heard, think of what else you needed at the time. Did you need someone to hold you while you cried? If so, put your arms around yourself and imagine this person is holding you now. Take time to comfort yourself with a warm blanket or a cup of tea or by holding a comforting object.

Many clients report that they either felt like crying or actually broke down sobbing after doing this exercise. Here are some things my clients have said:

- ❀ "There was no one there at the time to comfort me. I was all alone. I wish there had been someone there to say these words to me then."

- ❀ "That's all I ever wanted—just to be validated—just to have someone tell me they believed me and they understood how terrible it was for me, how hurt I was."

- ❀ "There wasn't anyone to tell me those words at the time, but imagining that a kind, loving person was saying them now makes it almost seem as if I had actually heard those words at the time. I feel comforted somehow."

❀ "I wanted to hear from my father that he was going to protect me from then on....So I imagined he was saying that to me and suddenly I felt safer."

If you have difficulty arriving at the right words when doing the above exercise, it may help you to read the compassionate statements that some of my clients wish they had heard at the time. Please read through the list slowly, pausing for a deep breath to take each item in.

❀ It wasn't your fault. You were an innocent child.

❀ This experience doesn't define you. You are so much more than this.

❀ You didn't deserve to be treated like this. No child deserves this.

❀ You were not a bad child. No child is perfect.

❀ You didn't do anything wrong.

❀ You were a sweet and loving child. You didn't deserve to be abused like this.

❀ This wasn't discipline or punishment—this was abuse and torture.

❀ You didn't ask for this. You didn't want it.

❀ Even though your body responded to the touch, it doesn't mean you wanted it.

You will probably notice that some of these statements resonate with you more than others. Write those that you had the most positive reaction to on a card or in a journal, and return to them again and again.

I hope you have been touched by some of the compassionate words I've shared with you or by the words of compassion that you yourself created and imagined receiving. I hope you've been able to allow these words to wash over you like warm, soothing water and that you have been comforted by them. And I hope they will help you to be willing and able to take in words of compassion that you may receive from other people in the future. This leads us to the next step: telling someone you trust about your abuse.

Part 3: Tell Your Story to a Compassionate Other

It can be very frightening to think of telling someone else about the abuse you experienced as a child. You may be afraid of being judged or of not being believed, especially if the abuse was extreme or unusual. You may also feel concerned that the person you tell will never see you in the same way as before. But telling someone close to you about the abuse can be a major step toward healing the shame you have surrounding the abuse. As the twelve-step saying goes, "You are only as sick as your secrets." This saying refers to the fact that secrets create shame and this shame makes us build up walls between ourselves and others. Not talking about the abuse also makes it so much easier to blame yourself and to continue to be plagued by shame. After all, you did nothing wrong. You did nothing to be ashamed of. Reminding yourself of this will make telling someone about the abuse a lot easier.

Choose someone to tell whom you can trust, and who is likely to hear your story without judgment. If you know someone is very judgmental of others, he is not the person to tell. It is also important to choose someone who is likely to believe what you tell her. If you know that a friend or family member has issues with people who say they have been abused, this is obviously not the person to tell. And if you know that a particular family member has made excuses for your abuser in the past or has an investment in not recognizing the truth about your abuser, this is not the person to tell. If at all possible, choose a person who you have personally experienced as being supportive and nonjudgmental and who is fairly informed about abuse issues.

Another reason some victims cite for not telling is that they do not want anyone to look at their abuser negatively. If this is your case, think about this a minute. This is your story to tell and you deserve to tell it. You deserve the healing that can come from bringing the abuse out into the light. If another consequence of telling is that your friend or family member learns for the first time that someone they care about abused you, this is not your problem. Your job is to take care of yourself and to continue to heal, not to protect your abuser. Your abuser has his or her own job when it comes to taking responsibility for his or her actions.

The optimum outcome would obviously be that the person you tell believes you, feels genuine compassion toward you, and is able to communicate this compassion in words or gestures (such as hugging you). You could also tell the person ahead of time that you have something important to tell her and that you don't want her to say or do anything. Telling someone, especially when it is the first time you open up to another person about the abuse, can be very difficult, so it is okay to take control of the situation if you need to. You can have a follow-up conversation at another time.

The more positive experiences you have telling friends and/or family members about the abuse, the more healing you will likely experience. If you can, go into the conversation with the mindset that it is the same as telling someone you are close to that someone stole your car or broke into your house. You would have no reason to feel shame if you were a victim of either one of these crimes, so why should you feel shame because you were the victim of the crime of child abuse?

When you do tell someone, try to take in any compassion you receive. Hopefully you have chosen a person who can be compassionate toward you, so let this be a healing experience. Take a deep breath and let the supportive words in. Don't cut the other person off by telling them that they shouldn't worry, that you are okay now, or that it wasn't so bad. And don't take care of his or her feelings: this is *your* time to receive understanding, support, and compassion. If you are fortunate enough to receive these things from the person, view them as gifts, gifts that you deserve.

If you are in a support group or recovery group, you will have an additional opportunity to tell others about your abuse experience. Most groups are set up so that all members have been advised as to how to react to someone telling a secret, especially when it involves abuse experiences, but make sure instructions have been given to the group to listen and not be judgmental.

In this chapter we have examined obstacles in receiving compassion from others. Hopefully reading about these has motivated you to stop letting them keep you from receiving the compassion you need in order to heal your shame. I encourage you to continue practicing allowing in good things. You deserve them.

We also explored what it might feel like if you had received the understanding, support, and compassion you deserved at the time of your abuse. Since you likely did not receive these at the time, it is important to receive them now. Don't minimize the healing power of these exercises by telling yourself that it's not the same. While nothing can be as healing as it would have been had someone actually been present to give you this compassion when you were a child, it is amazing how healing it can be to receive compassion today— even if it is in your imagination. Many clients have told me that imagining themselves hearing compassionate words from someone, especially someone they love, was powerful—almost as good as the real thing. And if you are able to tell someone today about the abuse and receive genuine compassion, it can be an incredibly powerful healing experience.

In the previous chapter, we began focusing on how you can process some of the feelings that inevitably come up as you face more of the truth about your abuse experiences. In the next chapter, we'll go a little deeper in helping you to process your feelings surrounding the abuse—especially the feelings of pain and grief.

6 Allowing Yourself to Feel Your Pain

Self-compassion is approaching ourselves, our inner experience, with spaciousness, with the quality of allowing which has a quality of gentleness. Instead of our usual tendency to want to get over something, to fix it, to make it go away, the path of compassion is totally different. Compassion allows.

—Robert Gonzales

Up to now, you've worked on overcoming some of your obstacles to compassion so you are in a better place to begin practicing self-compassion. An important aspect of self-compassion is allowing yourself to freely experience, process, and accept your emotions.

Sometimes we know intellectually that we were abused in certain ways, but have kept this awareness at arm's length, never really allowing ourselves to take in and *feel* the reality of how much we were harmed. Or—as may have happened for you as you read chapter 4—we eventually discover that we were abused in more ways than we originally thought. A positive result of recognizing on a deeper level how you have suffered because of the abuse is that some of the shame you once felt surrounding the abuse is replaced with anger or sadness. This process is essential to healing your shame.

Facing Your Pain

In chapter 4, I encouraged you to release some of your anger in healthy ways. But it's also important to realize that underneath your anger lie other emotions—including sadness, pain, and fear. It's painful to come face to face with the reality of what another person did to you—especially if that person was someone you loved or admired. It's painful to realize that someone you cared so deeply for could be so callous, cruel, or selfish. And it is painful to remember how hurt and betrayed you felt, and how frightened you were. In this chapter you will learn strategies that will help you to face this pain without becoming overwhelmed with it.

To begin with, it helps to understand the difference between *intellectually* recognizing how difficult things were for you and having real sympathy—or what psychologist Paul Gilbert, author of *The Compassionate Mind* (2009), calls "self-focused sympathy" (198)—for your distress. It's common to be able to recognize how difficult things were for you in a logical or dispassionate sense, without being able to have much sympathy for your suffering or to feel any kindness toward yourself for having had these experiences. It may be the case that you have not been genuinely moved by how painful your childhood was, how frightened you were as you were being abused, or how much pain you felt because of your abuse experiences.

When you have sympathy for yourself, it means you are emotionally open to your suffering—you are genuinely moved by the painful things you have experienced. This doesn't mean that you dwell on how bad it was, but that you feel kindness toward yourself for having suffered in the ways you have.

Many victims spent so much time holding themselves together and keeping going that they never really had a chance to process the trauma they experienced and the pain they suffered. Having sympathy for yourself means being able to recognize your pain without minimizing, denying, or dissociating from it. It also means that, when opportunities arise, you can work with your pain and share it with others (Gilbert 2009).

The Consequences of Shutting Off from Your Emotions

As humans we have an innate tendency to move away from pain, which can lead us to shut ourselves off from our emotions. But unless we face and process our emotions, we tend to either become slaves to them when they erupt out of us unannounced, or to disconnect from them entirely. Other consequences of avoiding your emotions can include:

- **You end up not really knowing yourself.** This is an important consequence, since it involves not understanding why you react to situations the way you do and not knowing the difference between what you think you want and what you really need.

- **You lose the good along with the bad.** When you shut down feelings like anger, fear, and sadness, you also shut down your ability to experience joy and love.

- **Your emotions become distorted or displaced.** People who attempt to avoid their feelings often end up projecting onto other people (accusing others of being angry, sad, or afraid when they're actually the ones experiencing these feelings) or displacing their anger (taking their anger out on innocent people).

- **It's exhausting.** You can distort and numb your emotions, but you can't eliminate them entirely. It takes a lot of energy to hold our feelings down, and the effort can leave you stressed and drained.

- **It damages your relationships.** The more you distance yourself from your feelings, the more distant you become from others, as well as yourself.

Why We Resist Feeling Sadness and Grief

I understand how difficult it is to allow your feelings surrounding the abuse to come up—especially your feelings of sadness and grief (that is, deep anguish felt in response to a significant loss). But just as you need to grieve when someone you love dies, you need to grieve the loss of your innocence, the loss of your love and trust, and perhaps the loss of the image you once had of the person who abused you. You need to feel the pain of what happened to you.

There are good reasons why we resist expressing our feelings of sadness and grief. Some people fear that if they begin to grieve they'll never stop. Others are afraid they will become depressed if they allow themselves to feel their pain. And others sense that they don't have the emotional strength to endure the pain. Still others fear that allowing themselves to grieve will transport them back to childhood and they will be unable to return to the present. These are all valid fears, so let's address them one by one.

1. **The fear of becoming overwhelmed with the pain and grief.** There is a reason why so many victims of childhood abuse resist feeling the pain surrounding the abuse—they sense that there is so much pain that they could easily become overwhelmed by it once they allow themselves to feel it. They sense that, because they have held in the pain for so long, it will create a flood of emotions once it's unleashed that they won't be able to contain. There can be some truth to this in the beginning. Once you allow yourself to release your pent-up pain, the tears may flow in huge waves. These waves of sorrow may last for quite a long time, and you may become afraid that you will never stop crying. But as a wise therapist once said when I asked her how long I would cry, "You'll cry until you have no more tears." Although it can be scary when you end up crying for a long time, the good news is that your body will take care of you. Your sobs may cause you to cough or choke—you may even need to throw up. But this is just your body's way of helping you clear both the physical and

emotional reminders of the abuse. Your body will not let you cry to the point where you are endangering yourself. You will either stop crying to catch your breath, or you will become so exhausted that you fall asleep.

2. **The fear of becoming so overwhelmed with grief that you become depressed.** Again, this is a very rational fear, although you are more likely to become depressed if you don't allow yourself to express your pain and grief. Nevertheless, we don't want you to get so stuck in your sadness and grief that you can no longer experience any good in the world. I am going to teach you techniques that will help you to move through your sadness instead of getting stuck in it—and, of course, if you feel you are getting stuck in your sadness or grief, please consult a psychotherapist or medical doctor.

3. **The fear that you do not have the emotional strength to endure the pain.** You know yourself better than anyone else. You know how fragile you are at any given time. You may not feel strong enough at this moment to face your pain, and that is okay. But if your pain and grief come up on their own, perhaps as you read this book, consider this: it has been my experience that clients aren't confronted with the truth about their abuse or the feelings that accompany it until they are ready. If you have been crying as you read this book, your body is telling you that you are sad and that you need to let out the tears. It is one thing to try to force yourself to grieve your losses associated with the abuse; it's another to hold back the tears once they start flowing spontaneously. And you may be a lot stronger than you think: Remembering what you have already survived can be a good reminder.

4. **The fear that you will get stuck in the past.** While this is another valid fear, there are ways of grounding yourself in the present so that you don't stay stuck in your past feelings or traumas. We will learn some of these in this chapter.

It's usually wise to seek a middle ground between facing your pain and avoiding it. If you feel particularly emotionally fragile one day, that may not be the day to focus on feeling your pain. But if you feel strong and fairly secure another day, that might be exactly the time to delve into the pain around an abuse experience. Another way to achieve balance is to allow yourself to face some of your pain, practicing self-compassion and mindfulness, and then rest for a few days until you can build up enough strength to process another piece of an abuse experience or incident of abuse.

There are techniques and strategies you can use to protect yourself so that your worst fears don't come true, and I am going to teach you some of these in this chapter. These include ways to confront and process your pain over having been abused, as well as ways to allow yourself to grieve your losses. I am confident you can engage in these processes without being further traumatized. If, however, you feel too overwhelmed or traumatized, I recommend you seek professional help to work through your pain.

Turning Toward Your Pain

You may notice that you are reluctant to try some of the exercises and processes in this chapter. This may only be a natural reaction to trying something new. However, it might be a signal that this is not an appropriate time for you to experience your pain. You and you alone will need to use your intuition to tell you whether you feel safe enough and emotionally strong enough to turn toward your pain.

Fortunately, there is a way to turn toward your pain without becoming overwhelmed by it. This is the practice of mindfulness. Mindfulness gives us the ability to accept painful thoughts and feelings in a balanced way. It may be, for you, a new and healthier way to deal with both the pain and suffering from your past abuse and the stress and suffering caused by the aftereffects of the abuse that you suffer today. Or you may know about the practice of mindfulness, and in fact already be practicing it. If this is the case, the following will serve as a review for you, and perhaps may offer you new ways to apply mindfulness specifically to healing your shame.

How Mindfulness Can Help You Grieve

How do you practice mindfulness? First and foremost, mindfulness involves *being in the present.* It has been said that the present moment is all we have. The past has already occurred and the future is yet to be. But we can become so lost in hopes or fears about tomorrow or regrets about yesterday that we miss the present.

In addition to learning how to pay attention in the present moment, we need to learn how to do so *without evaluation or judgment.* We need to use our conscious awareness and direct our attention to observe and *only* observe. So mindfulness entails observing what is going on in our field of awareness just as it is—*right here, right now.*

Acceptance is another aspect of mindfulness. When we respond to our emotional pain with acceptance instead of ignoring or trying to get rid of it, change can happen naturally. Acceptance, in this context, is not the same as feeling resigned, powerless, or hopeless, or sugarcoating reality. Rather, it refers to making a conscious choice to experience our sensations, feelings, and thoughts *just as they are.* When we practice acceptance in this way—giving up trying to control or manipulate our experience—we open the door to change.

Psychotherapists have long been engaged in the practice of helping clients overcome abusive and/or traumatic childhood experiences. Some simply listen compassionately to their clients' stories of abuse (which can be quite healing); others teach techniques that help clients deal with symptoms such as depression, anxiety, reactions to being triggered, self-harming behaviors, and flashbacks. Sometimes therapists try to help clients change distorted thinking or discard negative false beliefs about themselves caused by childhood abuse. These approaches are all helpful.

But many therapists are now discovering the benefits of helping their clients establish *a new relationship* with their thoughts and feelings, rather than directly challenging them. This new relationship is less avoidant and more accepting, compassionate, and aware (Germer 2009).

Mindfulness and self-compassion are tools to help you change your relationship to your painful thoughts and feelings engendered by abuse. There is a phrase currently in our culture: "leaning in." In the context of healing our emotions around the abuse we suffered, it means that instead of becoming defensive or fighting against feelings we think of as negative, we "lean in" to them—facing them and inviting them in. This describes what mindfulness and self-compassion can teach us. Slowly leaning in to your most difficult emotions with mindfulness and self-compassion—with open eyes and heart—can help you face them and transform your relationship to them. It's the process by which we get the most emotional relief.

Mindfulness is now seen as an important component in effective psychotherapy and emotional healing in general. When therapy goes well, clients develop an accepting attitude toward whatever they are experiencing in the therapy room, be it fear, anger, or sadness, and this compassionate attitude can then be transferred to daily life.

Taking a fresh look at difficult emotions like pain, anger, and fear can provide you with important information about what's happening inside you. Emotions become destructive—causing us greater mental or physical suffering—when we either cling to them or push them away. And emotions seem to get stronger the more we fight them. The healthier way to deal with difficult emotions is to hold them in an open, aware, self-compassionate way.

You can also change your relationship to your feelings by not judging an emotion or getting upset because you are feeling an emotion, telling yourself things like "I hate feeling like this" or "I shouldn't feel like this" or "I'm wrong to have this feeling." Instead you can work toward accepting the emotion with self-compassionate statements like "It's understandable that I would feel sad right now" or "I have a right to feel angry."

Mindfulness involves a focus on the experience of a person—sensations and thoughts as well as feelings. It also involves becoming more aware of and more "in" your experience by paying attention to the details of the world you exist in now as well as to your sensations, feelings, and thoughts as they emerge in your mind and body. Sometimes a mindful state happens spontaneously, as when you're struck by the beauty of a sunset. In that moment, you lose your sense of yourself and are in the flow of the moment, just being in and experiencing the now. It can also be practiced and cultivated, of course, as we'll explore with the exercises below.

To sum it all up, mindfulness involves:

- Being in the present

- Becoming more aware—paying attention to the details of your surroundings

- Focusing on your experience—sensations, thoughts, feelings

- Recognizing what is going on inside you, moment to moment

- Being accepting of what is going on, without criticizing or judging

When cultivated, mindfulness allows us to have a less reactive relationship to our inner experience.

Practicing Mindfulness

We'll start with an exercise that will keep you grounded and in the present while you practice the exercises and processes in the rest of the chapter. I recommend you use the following grounding technique before each exercise, whenever you find yourself triggered by a past memory, or when you find yourself dissociating, or leaving your body, which is common for trauma victims.

Exercise: Grounding

1. Find a quiet place where you will not be disturbed or distracted.

2. Sit up in a chair or on a couch. Put your feet flat on the ground. If you are wearing shoes with heels, take them off so you can have your feet flat on the ground.

3. With your eyes open, take a few deep breaths. Turn your attention to feeling the ground under your feet. Continue breathing and feeling your feet flat on the ground throughout the exercise.

4. Now, as you continue breathing, take a look around the room, scanning slowly, making sure you are actually seeing what is around you. Notice the colors, shapes, and textures of the objects in the room. If you'd like, turn your head as you scan for a wider view.

5. When your attention wanders, bring your focus back to feeling the ground under your feet as you continue to breathe and to notice the colors, textures, and shapes of the objects in the room.

This grounding exercise serves several purposes. It brings your awareness back to your body, which in turn can stop you from being triggered or from dissociating. It brings you back to the present, which is, again, a good thing if you have been catapulted back into the past by a memory or a trigger. Also, deliberately focusing your attention outside yourself by being visually involved in the world breaks a shame spiral and allows those feelings and thoughts to subside so they are not dominating your experience. And finally, grounding will prepare you to practice mindfulness.

Following is a very nonthreatening beginning exercise in mindfulness. You can't do it wrong, so don't worry about getting it right. The entire exercise should only take five minutes, but make sure you are in a quiet place with no distractions. (Electronics, in particular, should be turned off.)

Exercise: Mindfulness Practice

1. Sit comfortably and close your eyes. Take a few deep breaths and begin to notice what it feels like to be in your body. Just *be aware*

of and *be with* the physical sensations in your body as they come and go.

2. You need not pay attention to any particular sensation, but you may notice a feeling or sensation—a warmth in your hands, a tightness in your shoulders. Whether it is a pleasant or an unpleasant sensation, simply feel it and let it go. Just notice whatever feelings or sensations arise.

3. After about five minutes, gently open your eyes.

You may or may not notice that you are more in the present or more connected to your body after doing this exercise. Either way, it's okay. The point of this beginning practice is to help you become familiar with the practice of mindfulness.

Mindfulness and Anchoring

Mindfulness is a specific type of awareness that can keep you anchored safely in your body while you are experiencing strong emotions such as sadness, grief, or fear. When you are mindful, there is less need to escape unpleasant emotions. Mindfulness involves both knowing where your mind is from moment to moment and directing your attention in skillful ways. If you tried the exercise above, you may have already had a taste of what it's like to experience mindfulness, if momentarily. In a mindful moment, your mind is in a relatively receptive state and you are aware of sensations without needing to compare, judge, label, or evaluate them.

It becomes easier to focus if you are simply noticing what comes and goes, bringing your mind back to the moment whenever you find it wandering. But this requires practice, and overcoming some habits most people share. When we try to sit still for a few minutes and "allow our thoughts to come and go," we often find instead that we are unconsciously resisting our discomfort with the exercise, judging our discomfort or our apparent inability to stay focused, or allowing our mind to begin obsessing or fantasizing. It makes sitting still uncomfortable, even unbearable.

Because it's so difficult to let ourselves just observe and *be* without the automatic mental functions of labeling and judging taking over, the mind needs an *anchor*: something we can return to when our attention wanders or we have trouble letting our thoughts simply come and go. The most common anchor used in mindfulness practice is the breath, which is always there to return to. Paying attention to your breath is an excellent way to gather your attention and bring yourself into the present moment.

Unfortunately, victims of trauma often have a difficult time focusing on their breath. This can happen for several reasons. Victims of physical or sexual abuse may not like being reminded of their bodies, since this can bring back bad memories. For example, it is common for those who were sexually abused to be reminded of either the perpetrator's breathing or their own as they were being abused. Those who were held down, gagged, or confined in a small space may experience shortness of breath when they focus on their breathing. Those who suffer from physical pain due to flashbacks or being triggered by memories of the abuse may not want to focus on their body. And those who don't like how their body looks or who experience hatred of their body may find that focusing on their breath brings them too close to their bodies.

For these reasons, I recommend you find a different anchor. Your feet on the floor, as in the grounding exercise above, can act as your anchor. A physical object can also be an excellent anchor (a small stone, something given you by a loved one); just make sure it is readily available. For example, some people carry a small stone with them to help them become anchored or grounded whenever they experience a strong emotion or when they are triggered, or to use whenever they are practicing a mindfulness exercise.

Mindfulness and Painful Emotions

Now that you know the basics of mindfulness, let's utilize it to help you deal with your emotions related to your abuse experience—especially your pain, fear, and sadness.

The next time you are triggered or experience a strong emotion in relationship to the abuse, try to simply observe the emotion—where you feel it in your body, what sensations it elicits—without any kind of judgment or evaluation whatsoever. Refrain from labeling it "good," "bad," "painful," "pleasant," or any other evaluating word.

Try to notice the thoughts that go through your mind as you feel this emotion—the associations you have with it. Acknowledge if it's helpful or healthy, harmful or unhealthy, but don't judge it. Try to notice the opinions you have about this feeling and about the fact that you're feeling it. Let go of your opinions and simply feel. When you find yourself judging, don't judge your judging. Just set aside the judgment and move on.

Whenever we judge our emotions as "bad," the natural consequence is to feel guilt, shame, anxiety, and/or anger. The addition of these secondary feelings simply makes the distress more intense and intolerable. Often you will find that you can tolerate a distressing situation or painful emotion a lot better if you can refrain from feeling guilty or anxious about feeling the painful emotion in the first place. Think of occasions when you have had a secondary emotional reaction to a primary emotion (feeling angry or ashamed about getting angry, getting depressed about being depressed). Which causes you more pain or trouble—the primary emotion or the secondary one?

The key to managing your emotions is to experience them without inhibiting, judging, or distracting yourself from them. Being mindful of our emotions instead of fighting them or walling them off helps us let go of them. It takes practice, but it's worth it. The following exercise will help you experience your emotions without becoming overwhelmed by them. Try to use it any time you feel an intense emotion.

Exercise: The Wave

1. First, ground yourself (see the grounding exercise earlier in this chapter).

2. Begin by simply observing your emotion. Notice how it makes you feel. Notice what happens in your body as you feel the emotion.

3. Don't judge the emotion as good or bad. It simply is what it is.

4. Fully experience your emotion, but allow yourself to feel it as a wave, something that comes and goes. Try not to suppress the feelings or push the emotion away. However, don't hold on to the emotion or amplify it. Just let it rise up like a wave and then subside, in its own time.

This experience of simply witnessing an emotion—letting it arise, be, and recede—will put you in a better position, over time, to let go of the intense energy you may have invested in it. And once you are more detached from the emotion you can begin to let it go. It has served its purpose.

If, during the process of facing the abuse you experienced, or of grieving your losses, you begin to feel overwhelmed by your emotions, practice the following exercise.

Exercise: Detaching from an Emotion

1. First, ground yourself (see the grounding exercise earlier in this chapter).

2. Separate yourself from the emotion by telling yourself: "I am not my emotion."

3. Remind yourself that you don't need to act on your emotion.

4. Remind yourself of a time when you have felt differently—when you were not overwhelmed by this emotion or you were feeling another, less threatening emotion.

5. Remind yourself of a time you overcame the emotion.

By learning to observe your emotions, you learn to be separate from and also to be at one with them. Being separate from your emotions allows you to think about them and use coping strategies so you can be in better control of them. Being at one with your emotions allows you to identify them as part of you and not something outside you.

Combining Mindfulness with Self-Compassion

Self-compassion and mindfulness can work in tandem to help you learn to lean in to your pain and establish a new relationship with it. As Christopher Germer states in *The Mindful Path to Self-Compassion* (2009): "While mindfulness says, 'Feel the pain,' self-compassion says, 'Cherish yourself in the midst of the pain'" (89).

Mindfulness practice often leads naturally to self-compassion. However, in this section, we will focus on how to deliberately add self-compassion to the practice of mindfulness meditation. Mindfulness combined with self-compassion will help you experience emotional pain in safe doses instead of either avoiding it or allowing it to overwhelm you and your ability to focus and function. Self-compassion teaches us that instead of dealing with difficult emotions by fighting against them, we can acknowledge our pain and respond to it with kindness and understanding. Change and healing come naturally when we open ourselves to emotional pain and respond to it with self-compassion.

Connecting with Yourself

Oftentimes my clients have a difficult time feeling compassion for themselves for what they suffered around their abuse, usually because they feel very disconnected from themselves and their emotions. Some also have a distorted image of themselves when they were children, seeing themselves as older or more mature than they actually were, for example. And of course, shame can keep you from acknowledging just how horrible your abuse experiences were. If you are having difficulty feeling compassion for yourself, the following exercise may help you to connect more with yourself, with your feelings related to the abuse, and with the reality of the situation.

Exercise: What If It Had Happened to Someone Else?

1. First, ground yourself (see the grounding exercise earlier in this chapter).

2. Call to mind one of your abuse experiences.

3. Imagine that this abuse happened to your own child or to a child to whom you are emotionally connected.

4. Notice your emotional reaction as you imagine the abuse happening to this child.

5. Write down what your emotional reaction is to the thought of your own child or another beloved child being abused in this way.

6. Now write about the difference between how you reacted to the thought of the beloved child being abused and how you reacted to your own abuse. If you reacted differently, why do you think this is so? Write down the reasons.

You met John in chapter 2. He was the man who was molested by his grandfather. This is what he wrote after completing the above exercise: "I was astonished at how differently I reacted when I imagined my son being molested by my grandfather. I became enraged at my grandfather. I wanted to kill him! How dare he put one hand on my son! Then I thought about it and I wondered, why didn't I feel that same anger when I remembered my grandfather abusing me? In that moment I realized what the answer was. When I thought about the things my grandfather had me do, I always saw myself as being much older and more mature. That's why I always felt like I had a real part in it—that I made it happen as much as my grandfather did. That's why I always thought it was a natural outcome of the affection we felt for one another.

"But suddenly I saw myself as a little boy—as little and as innocent as my son. If someone approached my son and asked him to do those things, I wouldn't assume my son was old enough to choose that. I would see it as the adult taking advantage of my son, using his love for his grandfather to manipulate him into doing his bidding. For the first time since I've been working with you I finally understood what you've been trying to get me to see all along. I was an innocent victim. I was finally able to feel compassion for myself.

"I noticed that I felt truly sad about what happened to me. For the first time I let myself cry for myself, for what I went through and what I've had to go through all my life because of what my grandfather did to me."

Comforting Yourself

Imagining that the abuse happened to someone else can help you become more aware of how you feel about your own abuse experiences and connect with your own suffering. It can also remind you of what you most needed at the time.

Creating a self-compassion practice can strengthen your wish and your ability to alleviate your suffering. Spend a few minutes thinking about what you needed most at the time of your abuse. We touched on this in the previous chapter. Was it someone to listen to you, to comfort you? Was it someone to stand up for you, to protect you?

Allow yourself to be moved by how painful your abuse experience was. Just as it would have helped if there had been someone available to comfort you after the abuse, being available to yourself as you reexperience your pain (or, perhaps, as you allow yourself to feel it for the first time) can make your suffering more bearable.

- ❀ Imagine you're giving yourself now what you needed at the time of your abuse.

- ❀ If what you needed most was someone to listen to you, do that for yourself now. You can do this in your head, talking out loud to yourself, or you can write down your feelings about the abuse and then reread your words, really taking them in.

- ❀ If what you needed most was for someone to comfort you, do that for yourself now. Put your arms around yourself and lovingly rock yourself. Lie down and curl up in the fetal position. Sit in a rocking chair and gently stroke your arms.

- ❀ Give yourself compassion for how painful (frightening, humiliating) the abuse was. Comfort yourself with kind words such as: "I'm so sorry that happened to you"; "Poor little girl/boy"; or "You didn't deserve to be treated like that."

- ❀ If what you needed the most was someone to stand up for you or protect you, do that for yourself now. Say out loud such statements as "Stay away from him" or "She's just a child, stop expecting so much from her!"

Imagine how it would have felt if there had been someone available to hold or gently rock you after each of your abuse experiences. Being lovingly cared for in this way would not have made the abuse go away, but it would have soothed your pain in the moment.

Although you probably didn't receive this kind of loving touch at the time, it's not too late to provide it for yourself as you go through the grieving process. As you remember the pain of an abuse experience or are triggered by something in your environment, try the following exercise to give yourself this loving, soothing touch.

Exercise: Self-Soothing

1. First, ground yourself (see the grounding exercise earlier in this chapter).

2. Try the following: gently stroke your arm, face, or hair; gently rock your body; give yourself a warm hug.

3. Notice how your body feels after receiving each of these self-soothing touches. Does it feel calmer, more relaxed?

4. Notice which of these self-soothing touches feels the best to you. Do you have more positive associations with one than the others?

Don't allow your self-critical mind to talk you out of this exercise—it is not silly or self-centered to soothe yourself. It is a loving thing to do for yourself.

Supporting Yourself

It is often easier to tolerate difficult feelings and situations if we feel supported by others. The same is true when it comes to our relationship with ourselves. The kinder and more compassionate we are with ourselves, the more we can develop the courage to tolerate difficult things. The following exercise is another way to connect with your emotions related to the abuse and to provide support and nurturing toward yourself. Before you begin, find one or two photos of yourself as a child—photos that resonate with you, that remind you of your childhood. If you can find a picture of yourself taken around the time of the abuse, that would be ideal.

Exercise: The Self-Compassionate Letter

1. First, ground yourself (see the grounding exercise earlier in this chapter).

2. Take a long look at the picture or pictures you have chosen.

3. Notice the expression on your face, your posture, and any other cues that might be present to show how you were feeling at the time. You may notice that you look sad, afraid, or angry. Or you may not be able to see any such cues.

4. Notice how you feel as you look at the picture and as you think about what you were going through at the time of the abuse.

5. Write yourself a "self-compassion letter," in which you tell your child self how you feel now as you think about how you suffered as a child. Write it as if your adult self is addressing your child self.

6. Once you have completed your letter, read it out loud to yourself (or more accurately, to your child self). Allow yourself to take in these words of kindness, support, and compassion.

Emotions always express themselves in the body. If we can identify where we feel the emotion in our body, even intense emotions can be calmed. For example, when we feel grief or sadness, we may experience tension or hollowness in the chest area. When we are feeling anger, it is often as tension in the neck, shoulders, jaw, or hands, while fear is often felt as tension in the stomach. Shame is often felt as an empty feeling in the upper body or head.

Exercise: Softening into Your Feelings

1. The next time you are feeling an emotion related to the abuse (anger, sadness, fear, or shame), locate where that emotion resides in your body.

2. Once you have located the emotion, soften into it, rather than tensing up or resisting it.

3. Notice how your body feels as you soften into the feeling. Do you notice less tension? Are you more relaxed?

4. Continue to soften into the feeling.

The mindful and self-compassionate way to deal with painful feelings is to *befriend* them. This involves *softening* into physical or emotional distress instead of tightening up. And it involves being moved by the painful things you have experienced—being emotionally open to your suffering.

Self-compassion and mindfulness can go hand in hand, helping you experience the pain surrounding your abuse in ways that don't send you over the edge, catapult you back to the past, or keep you stuck in the past. By combining mindfulness with self-compassion, you can face your pain, experience it fully, comfort yourself, and open the doorway to real healing.

Hopefully we have confronted and eliminated many of the obstacles in the way of your accepting the concept of self-compassion. Now that you have laid the foundations of understanding and acceptance, and learned how you can soothe and comfort yourself as painful feelings about your abuse experiences arise, we'll move on to the next practice in my Compassion Cure program. Ahead you will find a structured system of skills, attitudes, and practices that, together, will allow you to heal more deeply from the effects of shame caused by your abuse.

Part III

Practicing the Five Aspects of Self-Compassion

My Compassion Cure program is made up of five components: self-understanding, self-forgiveness, self-acceptance, self-kindness, and self-encouragement.

In addition to alleviating shame, the Compassion Cure program is designed to teach victims of child abuse the following attitudes and skills:

- ❀ How to begin to view your symptoms and negative ways of coping—such as alcohol and drug abuse, sexual acting out or sexual addiction, or self-harm—as attempts to cope and as safety strategies (self-understanding).

- ❀ How to forgive yourself for harm you have caused yourself and others due to your abuse experiences (self-forgiveness).

- ❀ How to understand and experience the negative power of your self-criticism and refocus on self-compassion (self-acceptance).

- ❀ How to generate alternatives to your self-attacking thoughts, strengthening neural pathways that stimulate inner support and warmth (self-acceptance and self-kindness).

- ❀ How to create a nurturing inner voice to replace a cold, critical, bullying inner voice (self-acceptance and self-kindness).

- ❀ How to generate compassionate feelings for yourself and soothe yourself in positive ways (self-kindness).

- ❀ How to replace self-criticism with self-kindness (self-kindness).

- ❀ How to be supportive and encouraging of your efforts to change instead of trying to force or bully yourself into making changes (self-encouragement).

- ❀ How to identify and focus on your strengths, positive attributes, and skills (self-encouragement).

- ❀ How to develop appreciation for yourself and pride in yourself (self-encouragement).

- ❀ How to practice accountability versus self-blame, self-correction versus self-criticism (self-encouragement).

Kristin Neff was one of the first people to do research on self-compassion. Based on that research, and drawing from social psychology and Buddhist tradition, she divided self-compassion into three core components: self-kindness, common humanity, and mindfulness. "First it requires *self-kindness*, that we be gentle and understanding with ourselves rather than harshly critical and judgmental. Second, it requires recognition of our *common humanity*, feeling connected with others in the experience of life rather than feeling isolated and alienated by our suffering. Third, it requires *mindfulness*—that we hold our experience in balanced awareness, rather than ignoring our pain or exaggerating it. We must achieve and combine these three essential elements in order to be truly self-compassionate." (Neff 2011, 41)

I agree that for the average person these three components are essential in order to become truly self-compassionate. But based on my years of specializing in working with both victims and abusers, I believe the situation is somewhat different for victims of child abuse.

First of all, due to the amount of debilitating shame victims of child abuse experience, being able to practice self-kindness is extremely difficult. I would go so far as to say that practicing self-kindness is nearly impossible for many former victims until they first decrease the amount of shame they experience. This is because most victims don't believe they deserve self-kindness.

Therefore, in order for you to be willing and/or able to begin to practice self-kindness, you will need to practice what I consider to be three prerequisites: *self-understanding, self-forgiveness,* and *self-acceptance.* Without these prerequisites, most victims of child abuse will have neither the motivation nor the ability to practice self-kindness. Once former victims come to better understand that they were not to blame for the abuse, and to realize that many of the negative behaviors they engaged in were the only way they could cope with the abuse and/or function in the world, they tend to be more likely to accept and forgive themselves. Then and only then will they truly begin to practice self-kindness.

Self-encouragement is an essential component of self-compassion for victims of child abuse because, without it, you will likely slip back into old habits of judging yourself harshly and focusing on your so-called failures rather than your accomplishments.

While acknowledgment of their common humanity is important for victims of child abuse, I believe that the experience of child abuse really does separate its victims from the general population. So while victims of child abuse do share experiences with everyone else in the world, they also have unique experiences that need to be addressed; I'll do so in the chapters on self-understanding and self-forgiveness.

I incorporate the concepts of mindfulness and common humanity throughout the program. They support us through all our efforts to understand, forgive, accept, encourage, and be kind to ourselves as we grow in our ability to be self-compassionate.

7   Self-Understanding

The events of childhood do not pass,
but repeat themselves like seasons of the year.

—Eleanor Farjeon

Self-understanding is the first, and one of the most important, of the five components of the Compassion Cure program. Only by gaining self-understanding will you be able to relieve yourself of your burden of shame and stop both blaming yourself for the abuse and being so critical and judgmental of yourself. Without self-understanding you will find it difficult if not impossible to practice the other four components of self-compassion.

Like many who were abused in childhood, you may not only be overwhelmed with debilitating shame concerning the abuse itself, but also with shame concerning ways you have harmed yourself and others. This shame can interfere with your being able to feel self-compassionate. For this reason, self-understanding can actually be the key that opens the door to self-compassion. Once you come to understand yourself—including the motives and reasons for your more troubling behaviors—you'll find it easier to practice self-compassion.

Without self-understanding, those who were abused in childhood tend to continue putting themselves down for their mistakes and shortcomings instead of making the all-important connection between their current behavior and the abuse they experienced. I am not encouraging you to make excuses for problematic behavior, but without understanding why you have acted as you have, you will not only continue to experience debilitating shame and blame yourself unnecessarily; you will have a more difficult time letting go of the troubling behaviors.

Those who were abused in childhood are particularly hard on themselves. They have unusually high expectations of themselves, and they chastise themselves unmercifully when they make mistakes, especially when their behavior harms another person. And they seldom, if ever, search compassionately for reasons why they may have behaved as they did. Instead, they tend to have a "no excuses" policy regarding their own behavior. (Interestingly, they often don't have the same policy regarding the behavior of others, frequently making excuses for others' insensitive or abusive behavior.)

This is very sad when you think about it. As a victim of childhood abuse, you no doubt experienced sometimes horrendous pain and suffering at the hands of your parents or other adults. Yet you not only won't allow yourself to acknowledge your suffering but expect yourself to walk away from the abuse unscathed—to move on with life without receiving any help or healing.

Unfortunately, there is a huge price to pay for this way of thinking. First, if you were a victim of childhood abuse, you were traumatized by the experience. You may not have been aware of it at the time, but you were. And while you may not be aware of how the trauma affected you, it did nevertheless. As a comparison, let's say you were in a plane crash, and fortunately you could walk away and your physical injuries are now healed. But the experience of the crash was in itself traumatic. There were the moments leading up to the crash: the realization that your life was in danger, the fear of what was going to happen. Then the crash itself: the terror and pain of the physical impacts, the overwhelming sights, sounds, and smells.

Even though you were able to walk away from the crash, you would expect to carry the experience of the trauma with you, right? You'd replay the crash over and over in your head, remembering everything you experienced throughout the whole episode. You might expect yourself to be in shock long after the trauma, and to suffer from post-traumatic stress symptoms—nightmares, fear of airplanes, even terror responses when you hear airplanes passing over you—for quite some time to come. It would make sense to you that you would have suffered emotional and psychic wounds as well as physical injuries.

The same is true of children who experience childhood abuse and/or neglect. In addition to debilitating shame, you have carried the memories of the trauma and the stress that these memories continue to create. And these post-traumatic symptoms take their toll.

I have often found myself explaining to clients that I have actually never met a victim of childhood abuse who didn't react to the abuse with problematic behaviors—abusing alcohol or drugs, sexual acting out, sexual or other addictions, self-harm, abusive behavior toward loved ones, or a pattern of staying in abusive relationships. These behaviors just seem to come with the territory.

My hope for you is that instead of viewing yourself as a bad person because you have reacted to the trauma of your childhood abuse in sometimes troubling ways, you will come to understand yourself better with the information given in this chapter. This will in turn allow you to become less critical of yourself, as you come to recognize that the negative things you have done do not represent who you are at your core. Rather, they are the ways you learned to cope with the trauma you experienced. My further hope is that this self-understanding will help you begin to treat yourself in far more compassionate ways, and that as you come to realize how common it is for victims to react as you have, you'll feel less alone.

Throughout this chapter, I'll encourage you to make the important connection between your current (and past) behavior and your trauma experiences. Making this connection will help you become more compassionate toward yourself and less impatient, judgmental, and angry about your behavior.

Post-Traumatic Stress Disorder

Post-traumatic stress disorder or PTSD is a severe anxiety disorder with characteristic symptoms that develop after the experience of extreme trauma—such as the threat of severe injury or death to oneself or to someone else, or of a violent assault on one's own or another's physical, sexual, or psychological integrity, that overwhelms one's ability to cope.

People who suffer from PTSD often relive the experience through nightmares and flashbacks, have difficulty sleeping, and feel detached and estranged, and these symptoms can be severe enough and last long enough to significantly impair the person's daily life. PTSD is marked by clear biological changes as well as psychological symptoms. It is complicated by the fact that it frequently occurs in conjunction with related disorders such as depression, substance abuse, and problems of memory and cognition.

PTSD symptoms tend to fall into three major categories: reexperiencing, avoidance, and hyperarousal. *Reexperiencing symptoms* include flashbacks (reliving the trauma over and over, often accompanied by physical symptoms like sweating or a racing heart), bad dreams, and frightening thoughts. *Avoidance symptoms* include avoiding places, events, or objects that are reminders of the experience; emotional numbness, strong guilt, depression, or worry; loss of interest in activities that were enjoyable in the past; trouble remembering the traumatic event. *Hyperarousal symptoms* include being easily startled, feeling tense or "on edge," difficulty sleeping, and having angry outbursts.

As you read the above, you may have been surprised to realize that many of the symptoms you suffer from are actually symptoms of PTSD—that you have been suffering from PTSD for years. This realization may bring you some comfort in that finally, you're able to understand some aspects of your behavior and explain them to others. This can be the beginning of your gaining self-compassion for your suffering.

In some cases of PTSD, the symptoms can actually become more debilitating than the trauma. For example, intrusive memories are mainly characterized by sensory episodes rather than thoughts. These episodes aggravate and maintain PTSD symptoms, since the individual reexperiences trauma as if it were happening in the present.

Many victims of childhood abuse can be diagnosed with PTSD, and many are plagued by these sensory episodes. My client Melanie frequently feels the presence of her brother, who brutally sexually abused her starting when she was three years old. Sometimes she wakes up in the middle of the night in terror because she thinks she feels him sitting on her bed. Other times, when she is in the shower, she senses him coming into the bathroom. Each time these episodes occur, Melanie is re-traumatized by the experience. It's no wonder people with PTSD look for any way possible to cope with these episodes.

PTSD is further associated with impairment of a person's ability to function in social and family life, including occupational inability, marital problems, family discord, and difficulties in parenting. Those with PTSD are particularly vulnerable to repeating the cycle of violence for the following reasons:

1. Many people with PTSD turn to alcohol or drugs in an attempt to escape their symptoms.

2. Some characteristics of PTSD can create abusive behavior, including irritability (extreme oversensitivity to noise or minor stimuli), explosive behavior, and/or trouble modulating and controlling anger.

3. Some characteristics of PTSD can create victim-like behavior, including helplessness and passivity, self-blame and a sense of being tainted or evil, and attachment to trauma (relationships that resemble the original trauma are sought).

Not all victims of childhood abuse suffer from PTSD, but those who have experienced interpersonal victimization at home or in the community have been shown to be at a very high risk for PTSD. Studies have shown that childhood abuse (particularly sexual abuse) is a strong predictor of the lifetime likelihood of PTSD.

Complex Trauma

Children who are exposed to multiple and/or chronic traumas, usually of an interpersonal nature, suffer a unique set of symptoms that can differ somewhat from those of PTSD. These children suffer from serious behavioral, interpersonal, and functional problems, such as a disrupted ability to regulate their emotions, behavior, and attention. This phenomenon is known as *complex trauma*. Like those who suffer from PTSD, victims of complex trauma often attempt to cope with their problems by self-medicating, and thus often become alcoholics, drug addicts, or compulsive overeaters, or suffer from other addictions. Those who have experienced such trauma often repeat the cycle of abuse—either becoming abusers or continuing to be victimized. The name for this is *intergenerational transmission of trauma*.

Rates of major depression, anxiety disorders, substance abuse, and personality disorders are especially high among this group (even more so than among those who suffer from PTSD). Unless victims are able to recover from the adverse effects of trauma, these effects may continue throughout their lives—most significantly in the area of interpersonal relationships.

In addition to suffering from most of the problems that those with PTSD suffer, victims of complex trauma tend to experience:

- Extreme behaviors (self-injurious behaviors such as cutting, head banging)

- Extreme sexual acting out (addictions to illicit sex or pornography; reenacting sexual trauma)

- Creating high-risk or painful situations in order to counteract feeling numb or dead inside (self-harming behaviors)

- Sudden outbursts of anger

- Suicidal ideation or suicide attempts

- Extreme risk-taking behavior

❀ Reenacting unhealthy relationships

If you suffered multiple traumas in childhood (for example, you were neglected or emotionally abused by your parents, you were sexually abused as a child over several years' time, and you were raped when you were an adolescent) you likely suffer from complex trauma. Note which items above describe your symptoms.

Trauma-Sensitive and Trauma-Informed

The terms "trauma-sensitive" and "trauma-informed" refer to more helpful and compassionate ways of perceiving the behavior of people who have been traumatized. A *trauma-sensitive approach* challenges the way we tend to look at trauma victims, encouraging them to treat themselves (and be treated by professionals) with more dignity, respect, and compassion than they usually do. The term *trauma-informed* implies that victims and service providers alike have been educated or trained in the consequences of trauma. It involves understanding, anticipating, and responding to the issues, expectations, and special needs of a person who has been traumatized.

By treating yourself and your symptoms in trauma-sensitive and trauma-informed ways, you increase your ability to treat yourself in a more compassionate way. This perspective frames many post-traumatic symptoms as *understandable* attempts to cope with or adapt to overwhelming circumstances, and is therefore more empathetic and more potentially empowering for victims.

The primary goal of a trauma-sensitive or trauma-informed approach is to help you better understand the role trauma has played in shaping your life. More specifically, there is a focus on helping you recognize that many of the behaviors you are most critical of in yourself (and are criticized for by others) are actually coping mechanisms or attempts at self-regulation. These include efforts to cope with high levels of anxiety—with, for example, smoking, drinking, and self-harm—and behaviors that result from an inability to self-soothe in a healthy way, like alcohol and drug abuse or overeating.

Below are some of the principles of a trauma-informed way of thinking; I encourage you to recall these as you continue to focus on healing your shame and any other effects of the abuse you suffered.

- ⚘ The impact of trauma narrows a victim's life, constricts her choices, and undermines self-esteem, taking away control and creating a sense of hopelessness and helplessness.

- ⚘ Many behavioral problems victims experience are actually adaptive responses to trauma. So symptoms—including troubling behaviors—need to be viewed as attempts to cope with past trauma, and as *adaptations* rather than *pathology*.

- ⚘ Substance use and certain psychiatric symptoms may have evolved as coping strategies at a time when options were limited. Every symptom helped a victim in the past and continues to help in some way in the present.

- ⚘ The focus should be on what happened to the person rather than what is wrong with the person.

- ⚘ Victims are doing the best they can at any given time to cope with the life-altering, frequently life-shattering aftereffects of trauma.

With this perspective, instead of blaming yourself for your efforts to manage traumatic reactions, you can begin to recognize the adaptive function of your symptoms. For example, drinking and other forms of substance abuse often arise out of a victim's efforts to cope with high, sometimes intolerable levels of anxiety. Recognizing this and having compassion for yourself is a significant step toward change. Next, you can focus on learning strategies that help you feel more comforted and in control, such as writing in a journal, taking a warm bath, applying a cool washcloth to your forehead, or practicing grounding exercises or deep breathing—all of which can help with self-soothing deficits.

The benefits of trauma-informed thinking include:

❀ It transforms you from being "bad" to being hurt (or wounded), opening the door for a more empathetic, constructive attitude toward yourself.

❀ It externalizes your problem. You can see yourself as basically good, with some problems that have intruded on your life but do not represent your core being. The symptoms are the problem, not you.

❀ It normalizes. Victims tend to feel they are not normal—bad, stigmatized, broken, sick. Trauma-informed thinking helps you see yourself as having normal and reasonable (understandable) reactions to unfortunate events.

❀ It emphasizes strengths and resources. Because you're likely to be critical of yourself, especially of the problematic ways you have sometimes behaved due to the abuse, it's important to look for your strengths and give yourself credit for them. (We'll focus on this in chapter 11.)

❀ It mobilizes victims to discover healthier and more productive coping strategies.

When you come to understand where the problem comes from, when you can feel compassion for your suffering, you will begin to feel more capable, be more empowered to solve the problem, and have more hope for improvement.

Connecting Behavior and Experience

Making the connection between your behavior and your trauma experience will help you become more compassionate and less impatient, judgmental, and angry at your behavior. Some of the problematic behaviors that are most common in victims of childhood abuse are listed below, with the forms of abuse most likely to have caused them. This list is not comprehensive, but will merely help you begin to understand the connection between troubling behaviors and the abuse you experienced.

Eating disorders. Eating problems such as bingeing, compulsive overeating, and emotional eating are especially common among those who were emotionally abused. These issues arise as a way to cope with profound feelings of emptiness, loneliness, depression, agitation, or other forms of distress.

Self-injurious behavior. Behaviors like cutting, intentionally self-inflicting cigarette burns, or head banging almost universally emerge originally as attempts to cope with severe abuse (long-term sexual abuse, sexual abuse by multiple perpetrators, severe neglect and abandonment, sadistic or severe physical abuse).

Difficulties with sexual adjustment. Difficulties such as a tendency to sexualize relationships, becoming hypersexual or avoiding sexual contact, or alternating between these two extremes usually stem from experiences of childhood sexual abuse.

Alcohol abuse and drug abuse. Alcohol abuse and drug abuse are common coping mechanisms for survivors of all forms of childhood abuse, including neglect and abandonment, verbal abuse, emotional abuse, physical abuse, and sexual abuse. However, there has been more research connecting alcohol and drug abuse to physical and sexual abuse than to other forms of abuse.

Using Substances to Manage the Impact of Abuse

A person who has been emotionally, physically, and/or sexually abused in childhood has to contend with powerful emotions and, often, interpersonal chaos. Regrettably, some victims discover they can ease the pain left by the trauma by abusing alcohol or certain drugs.

It can be helpful to see the connections between the feelings you are trying to manage and the substances you choose to use and abuse. The explanations that follow don't constitute excuses for using, but they can help you place your substance use in context and begin to consider alternative ways you might manage some of your symptoms and feelings. Following are some common trauma symptoms and the drugs victims tend use to ease or manage them.

Depression. Many victims report feeling hopeless and despairing about their lives and their prospects for ever feeling good again. Drugs such as cocaine, which elevates mood for a short time, may seem like a panacea for victims who experience prolonged depression.

Anxiety. Trauma leaves victims feeling anxious and fearful. In the short term, they may be worried that more abuse will be forthcoming, and in the long term they may experience a pervasive sense of dis-ease and worry. Alcohol and some tranquilizers such as benzodiazepines can lessen the anxiety of a victim who feels chronically on edge.

Inner turmoil and pain. Victims who are plagued by flashbacks and recurring memories of the abuse may feel that the intensity of their experience is too great to bear. They may seek drugs that induce forgetting and tend to dull or numb all sensation. They are at especially high risk for choosing opiates or alcohol to dull the pain.

The absence of all feeling. While some victims feel too much, others report that the abuse left them unable to feel anything at all. They report an absence of all sensations, from sexual arousal to everyday happiness or sadness. For these victims, any substance that produces an increase in sensation is appealing. They may find themselves drawn to cocaine or amphetamines for an immediate rush or to hallucinogens for a heightening of experience.

Passivity. A long-term consequence of the abuse for some victims is the absence of any motivation or ability to stand up for themselves. They may report that they see no choice other than to submit when someone is aggressive or intimidating toward them, and they wish they could feel legitimate anger or assertiveness. Drugs such as alcohol or PCP that release and enhance anger may have a particular appeal for victims who feel they are too passive.

Excessive anger and rage. When victims acknowledge what was done to them at the hands of an abuser, they may experience overwhelming feelings of anger coupled with a desire for retaliation. If the abuser is no longer living or is inaccessible due to illness or distance, a victim may find she feels angry but has no legitimate outlet for her rage. In some cases she will turn to drugs that leave her feeling less angry and more accepting or mellow—alcohol, marijuana, or opiates.

Holly's Story: Using Alcohol to Soothe Anxiety

Holly used alcohol to soothe the anxiety she experienced as a result of her childhood abuse experiences, and as a way of managing her constant flashbacks. "I hate myself," she told me. "I've really screwed up my life because of my drinking. I've lost my kids, my husband, my job—everything I loved. You'd think after all I've lost I'd stop drinking—but I don't. What's wrong with me? What is it going to take for me to put down that damn booze?"

Holly was not unlike many of my clients who constantly beat themselves up for their behavior, and who seem to be clueless about why they act as they do.

"Do you have any idea why you drink?" I asked Holly gently. "And why it is so difficult for you to stop?"

"Yeah, I know why I drink. I drink because I like the way it makes me feel. And I don't stop because I'm weak and lazy and stupid."

"Well, I think you've hit on something there—not the part about you being weak and lazy and stupid; I don't believe that. But the part about how it makes you feel. Can you describe the feeling you get from drinking?"

"Yeah, it feels good to be drunk. I don't have to think about anything. Everything seems softer—it takes away all the hard edges."

"What would you have to think about if you weren't drunk?" I asked.

"Oh, everything—how I've screwed up my life, mostly."

"Yes, but before you screwed up your life. What didn't you want to think about then?"

It took a while but eventually I got Holly to talk about her childhood—the real reason she preferred being drunk.

Holly had been physically and sexually tortured by her father from the time she was six until she ran away from home at sixteen. Because of the abuse, she experienced flashbacks almost daily. Being drunk was the only way Holly had found to block out the memories, at least temporarily. When she drank she felt a sense of peacefulness and euphoria she couldn't experience any other way. Far from being stupid, Holly had found a clever (albeit self-destructive) way to self-medicate.

Once I explored with Holly the fact that she actually had a good reason to drink and that she was doing the best she could to cope with her childhood trauma, she was able to become less critical of herself. I then explained to her that while getting drunk helped her to block out memories and cope with her flashbacks, this coping mechanism was maladaptive in that it did not help her heal from the abuse. In fact, her drinking resulted in more trauma (for example, the loss of her children). Maladaptive behaviors such as alcohol abuse often cause out-of-control responses, including deep shame, distorted thought processes, and behavior that results in negative life consequences.

An Opportunity for Self-Understanding

If you have an alcohol or drug dependency, it is important to realize that it is very likely you are using the substance to cope with trauma symptoms. This understanding can help you to be less critical of yourself and also motivate you to discover and practice more effective ways of coping.

I asked Holly to complete the following sentence in a way that applied to her situation: "Given my history of abuse, it is understandable that _____."

Here are her responses:

Given my history of abuse, it is understandable that *I would try to find some way to block out the pain.*

Given my history of abuse, it is understandable that *I started drinking at such an early age.*

Given my history of abuse, it is understandable that *I would drink excessively.*

Given my history of abuse, it is understandable that *I would have a difficult time giving up drinking.*

I suggest you use the same sentence stem, completing the sentence as many times as you can think of responses.

Exercise: It Is Understandable

Given my history of abuse, it is understandable that _____.

Grounding

When I shared more effective ways of coping with Holly, she found the grounding technique I taught you in chapter 6 to be highly effective in managing her flashbacks. Grounding is a powerful yet simple strategy to help you manage and detach from emotional pain, such as memories of the trauma or flashbacks, dissociating, or panic episodes. The goal is to shift attention away from negative feelings and toward the external world. Grounding is particularly powerful because it can be used in any situation where you are caught in emotional pain or triggered, and it can be done anytime, anywhere, without anyone noticing it.

Please note that grounding is not a "relaxation technique"—in fact, it is often a more effective tool for centering victims than such techniques are. Some victims with PTSD actually become more anxious when they are guided through conventional relaxation techniques. Closing their eyes can lead to dissociation for some victims, and focusing on breathing—or even hearing the word "relax"—may be triggers that remind them of sexual abuse.

Most victims report that they feel more "present" after practicing grounding. In fact, many are surprised to realize that they are "out of their body" (dissociated) more often than they realize. Practice grounding whenever you are extremely anxious, when you are having flashbacks or traumatic memories, and whenever you feel you are dissociated.

Putting Your Behaviors in Context

A better understanding of why you have adopted certain behaviors as a way of coping with the abuse you experienced will hopefully lead to less shame about troubling or problematic behavior and allow you to feel less critical of yourself. The following exercise will help you build on your self-understanding.

Exercise: The Connection Between the Abuse and Your Behaviors

1. Make a list of your most troubling behaviors—the things you have done that cause you the most shame (like abusing alcohol or drugs, sexual acting out, abusive behavior).

2. Take a close look at each behavior and see if you can find the connection between it and your abuse experiences. Use the sentence stem I gave Holly, to say something like: "Given my history of abuse, it is understandable that I would behave like this."

3. Once you have made this all-important connection and stated that it is an understandable one, check to see if you feel more compassion for yourself and your suffering.

4. The next time you find yourself behaving in an unhealthy or self-destructive way, instead of chastising yourself for the behavior (or for the desire to act in an unhealthy way), repeat the sentence, or simply say to yourself, "I understand why I'm acting like this."

Repeating the Cycle of Abuse

Thus far we have discussed the reasons why victims use such coping mechanisms as substance abuse, self-harm, and sexual and other addictions. In this section we'll focus on another reason victims carry around a tremendous amount of shame: because their behavior hurts other people.

Sadly, no one gets through an abusive or neglectful childhood unscathed; even sadder is that no one escapes without somehow perpetuating the cycle of violence. In many cases, those who were abused or neglected become both abusers and victims throughout their lifetimes. Research clearly shows that those who have been abused either absorb abuse or pass it on. In the past twenty-five years, studies on abuse and family assaults strongly suggest that abused children are at greater risk of becoming abusers themselves and that child victims of violence are far likelier to become violent adults. Individuals with a history of childhood abuse are four times more likely to assault family members or sexual partners than are individuals without such a history. Females who have a history of being abused in childhood are far more likely to continue being victimized as adults.

Even the most well-meaning person will find himself exploding in the same kind of rages he witnessed or experienced as a child. His rage is likely to surface when he drinks too much, feels provoked, or is reminded of or triggered by memories of his own abuse. Or, the reverse may be true: if she was battered as a child or witnessed her mother being abused, a girl may grow up to marry a man who physically abuses her or her children. She will be rendered helpless—unable to defend herself or to leave, just as her mother was before her.

All too often a sexually abused male (or, less often, a female) will sexually abuse his own children. If he marries a woman who was also sexually abused (which happens frequently), she will typically become what is called a silent partner—someone in such denial about her own abuse that she stands by while her own children are being molested. Sometimes victims of childhood sexual abuse who do not molest their own or other people's children are so afraid of the chance they might repeat the cycle that they cannot be physically affectionate toward their own children.

Generally, the trauma of childhood abuse appears to amplify gender stereotypes: men with histories of childhood abuse are more likely to take out their aggression on others, while women are more likely to be victimized by others or to injure themselves. In fact, the *cycle of violence* theory holds that physically abused boys are more likely to grow into physically abusive and violent men than their nonabused counterparts and that physically abused girls are more likely to become victims of abuse as adults (Herman 1997).

Rosa's Story: Continuing to Be Victimized

"I don't know what's wrong with me. I've put up with my husband physically abusing me for almost twenty years now. He's put me in the hospital three times and I lied to the doctors and the police each time. My family has completely given up on me—they've tried to help me so many times, but now they say it is just too painful to see my bruises. And my kids….God knows what I've done to them. My older son is as mean as his father and he treats me just like his father does, ordering me around, criticizing everything I do. My youngest son is as afraid of my husband as I am and he basically stays away from him. His older brother has been bullying and harassing him for years and now he's even being bullied at school. He begs me to leave his father but I still can't do it. I'm the poorest excuse for a mother…" This is how my client Rosa started her first session with me.

Research shows that not only were most battered women victims of either emotional, physical, or sexual abuse in childhood but most suffer from complex trauma, which we discussed earlier in this chapter (Herman 1997). This was the case with Rosa, who was severely physically abused as well as neglected by her mother when she was growing up. Rosa's mother was herself a battered woman, and Rosa witnessed her father brutally abusing her mother many times.

It was no coincidence that Rosa ended up marrying someone who would eventually batter her. Rosa's self-esteem was so damaged and she was so traumatized by her childhood that she could barely look people in the eye when she spoke to them. But Frank took a special interest in her and treated her with respect and kindness. They fell in love quickly and told each other everything, including how they had both been abused as children. It was the first time Rosa felt really seen by another person—the first time she felt heard and understood.

But just as Rosa's childhood abuse set her up to be battered, Frank's abuse history set him up to be a batterer. It wasn't long before Frank started exploding in rage whenever Rosa didn't meet his expectations. (It is common for victims of childhood abuse to have unreasonably high expectations of their partners, including having the expectation that their partners will make up for what they missed in childhood.)

Over time I was able to help Rosa understand why she had stayed with Frank, in spite of the fact that he had become so abusive to her. Not only had the continued abuse damaged her already low self-esteem even further, causing her to fear that she couldn't survive living without Frank, but she couldn't bear to leave the one person in her life who had understood and supported her concerning the abuse she had suffered. Rosa and Frank had a tremendous bond. She felt sorry for him—she knew why he acted the way he did and that he couldn't help it. How could she leave him?

An Opportunity for Self-Understanding

Battered women are frequently misunderstood even by those who are closest to them. Family and friends simply cannot see why they won't leave such a damaging situation. But I promise, based on my experiences working with abused women and men for over thirty years, there is always a good reason and it typically has something to do with an abusive childhood. If you are currently the victim of emotional or physical abuse and have been unable to leave the situation, even though you know it is damaging to you and/or your children, I hope Rosa's story can help you understand yourself better. The following exercise may also help.

Exercise: Why Can't I Leave?

1. Make a list of all the reasons you are unable to leave the situation or end the relationship (like a fear of being alone or of not being able to support your children, or the belief that your partner will commit suicide if you leave him or her).

2. Now search your childhood background for connections in terms of the reasons you listed above. For example, you may have listed a fear of being alone because as a child you were often left home alone with no one to care for you. If you listed a fear of not being able to support your children, it may be because your father abandoned the family and you went through a time when you didn't have enough to eat. The belief that your partner might commit suicide could come from the fact that your father either threatened or actually committed suicide when your mother left him.

Repeating the Cycle by Becoming Abusive

While it's difficult for most of us—including the victim herself—to understand why a battered woman stays in an abusive relationship, it's even harder to understand why someone would abuse another human being in such an atrocious way. With Rosa and Frank, I provided a small window into one batterer's story. My client Ray's story gives more insight.

Ray's Story: Repeating What Was Done to Him

I saw Ray relatively early in my career. He had been required by law to seek counseling for physically abusing his wife. I was an intern at a batterer's intervention program at the time; and while I had compassion for abusers, just as I did for victims, I didn't have a complete understanding of why they abused. At that time, batterers were thought to have an anger management problem, not a shame management problem. Working with Ray was a gift to me, because he offered me a much deeper understanding of the batterer's plight than I otherwise would have experienced.

Ray presented himself the way many abusers do—he was defensive to the point of being argumentative and seemed completely closed to any help I might offer. He was convinced that the reason he abused his wife was because she refused to listen to him and that the solution to their problems was for her to do what he told her. While he understood he had to stop hitting her if he was going to stay out of jail, he couldn't see that it was wrong for him to treat his wife like property.

Gradually, over a period of weeks, I came to suspect that underneath all Ray's defensiveness and bravado was a great deal of shame. It took a while, but I eventually discovered that Ray's father had been severely emotionally abusive toward Ray when he was a child— extremely controlling and demanding. When he didn't meet his father's unreasonable expectations, his father would chastise him: "You're such a lazy bum. I don't know what's wrong with you. Anyone else could finish this job. I guess you're just too weak."

When I tried to get Ray to talk about how he felt about the way his father treated him, he tried to brush it off: "It wasn't any big deal. He did it for my own good."

But I was determined to help Ray begin to have compassion for himself, for what he had suffered. The best way I could do this was to show Ray compassion. "When you describe the way your father talked to you, it makes me feel angry," I told him. "He didn't have the right to talk to you that way, even if he was your father. I also feel very sad. It must have really hurt your feelings for him to be so cruel toward you and for him to attack your character that way. It sounds like you were doing the best you could, but it was never good enough for your father. I imagine you must have felt humiliated when he called you lazy and weak. I'm so sorry that it happened to you."

At first, Ray argued with me: "Well, he really needed that fence painted and I wasn't doing a good job."

"But do you think any kid your age could have completed the job in one day? Weren't your father's expectations too high?"

"He was just trying to teach me to be responsible."

"Yes, but did your father have to be so cruel to you? Did he have to call you names?"

Over the following months I continued working with Ray to help him begin to see that his father had been emotionally abusive toward him and that he felt horribly shamed and humiliated because of it. And I continued to offer him compassion for his suffering. Eventually, Ray began to acknowledge that perhaps his father had been too hard on him.

The next step was to encourage Ray to have compassion for himself. He began to recognize that he had been, after all, just a little boy and that his father's expectations were too high. He got to the point where he could tell me that for the first time in his life he didn't feel like a screw-up.

Relieved of some of his shame, Ray could afford to look at his own behavior more honestly. It wasn't long before Ray began to see how he did to his wife what had been done to him. He recognized that he insisted his wife do everything he demanded because he wanted to control her the way he had been controlled. And when she didn't comply he felt enraged because he once again felt shamed. "I needed to see myself as the man, as the boss. When she didn't do things exactly the way I wanted I felt like a failure."

By gaining self-understanding and connecting with his own suffering, Ray was able to have true compassion for his wife's suffering. By the time Ray left the program, I was no longer worried about him abusing his wife again—but of course, I couldn't be sure.

About six months later, Ray sent me this letter:

Dear Miss Engel,

I just want to tell you how much I appreciate the work you did with me. No one in my life has ever understood me the way you did. And no one has been so kind. That helped me feel that maybe I could be kind to myself. I learned so much from you. Mostly I learned that I didn't want to treat my wife and kids the way I was treated.

P.S. My wife wants me to thank you too.

Ray

An Opportunity for Self-Understanding

If you have become abusive I hope the story about Ray will help you remember that there is *always* a reason someone becomes an abuser. In fact, I have never known an abusive person who wasn't abused in some way. This isn't an excuse, just an explanation. As you have hopefully begun to realize, being understood and gaining self-understanding can be powerful healing tools.

The first step in preventing yourself from reenacting the abuse or neglect you experienced as a child or stopping behavior you have already begun is to make a clear connection between your current behavior and the behavior of your abusers. The following exercise will help you see more clearly how much your current behavior repeats your parents' or other abuser's behavior.

Exercise: What Do You Have in Common with Your Parents?

For this exercise you will need three or four pieces of paper.

1. On one piece of paper or on a journal page, write the ways your mother was or is neglectful or abusive toward you or others. Include attitudes and verbal comments as well as behaviors.

2. On a second piece of paper, list any of your father's behaviors, attitudes, or comments that were or are neglectful or abusive.

3. If you were raised by other adults (foster parents, grandparents, and so on) make a separate list of each of these people's behaviors and attitudes that were neglectful or abusive.

4. On another piece of paper, list the ways you have been neglectful or abusive toward your children, your partner, or anyone else in your life. No one else needs to read this list but you. Making this list will no doubt be difficult and painful, and you may attempt to lie to yourself or put it aside. If this happens, remind yourself of your resolve to heal yourself of your shame and break the cycle,

take a deep breath, and try again. Remember that as difficult as it is to write this list, it can make the difference between breaking the cycle or continuing it for another generation. And imagine how much more difficult it will be to face the damage you inflict if you aren't honest with yourself now.

5. Compare your lists. Notice the similarities between the ways you have been neglectful, or abusive, and the ways your parent(s) were neglectful or abusive toward you or others.

The Less Obvious Legacies of Abuse and Neglect

In addition to continuing the cycle of abuse, there are other more subtle legacies of abuse and neglect. For example, those with such a history are often unable to see partners, children, or even coworkers clearly. Instead they see them through a distorted lens of fear, distrust, anger, pain, and shame. They see ridicule, rejection, betrayal, and abandonment when it isn't there. Their low self-esteem causes them to be hypersensitive, taking things far too personally. And they will likely have issues with control, either needing to dominate others or being far too easily dominated by others. Those with a history of neglect or abuse are often unable to trust their partners. Instead they repeat the past dramas of their parents and perceive their partners as enemies, not allies. Those who become parents find it difficult to see their children's needs and pain without being reminded of their own. They also find it difficult to allow their children to make a mistake without taking it as a personal affront or a sign that they are not a good parent. In work environments, past dramas with parents and siblings get reenacted with bosses and coworkers. Think about the effect the neglect or abuse you experienced has had on you. In the following exercise, list or write about how it has affected the way you view yourself and the way you view others.

Exercise: Subtle Effects of Abuse and Neglect

The abuse has affected the way I view myself in the following ways:

_____

_____

The abuse has affected the way I view others in the following ways:

_____

_____

Practicing Self-Understanding

While some people are more resilient than others, the damage inflicted upon a victim of childhood abuse has long-term consequences, as we have discussed. Putting yourself down for behaving in such predictable and understandable ways is not going to help you stop negative and destructive behaviors. In fact, it will only make you feel worse about yourself and consequently less motivated to change. But gaining self-understanding will help. Self-understanding stops you from adding to the already overwhelming amount of shame you carry around with you, and it can also act as fuel to motivate you to grow and change.

One of the primary goals of self-understanding is for you to stop the constant self-judgment and focus instead on beginning to understand your faults and failures. Rather than blaming yourself for your mistakes or omissions, it is important that you begin to believe you had a good reason for your actions or your inaction. This is a huge step, but one that is essential if you are to begin ridding yourself of the debilitating shame that has burdened your life.

It is also a step you'll find yourself needing to take whenever you become too critical of yourself for your current or past behavior. Look to the exercises you've already done in this chapter. They will give you a survey of the kinds of behaviors that will crop up and cause you to criticize yourself. When this happens, remind yourself: "Given all I have experienced and suffered in my childhood, it's understandable I would have this symptom or exhibit this behavior." Or simply say, as calmly and compassionately as you can, "It's understandable why I do this." Over time, the self-understanding will sink in deeper.

As we've discussed, former victims tend to view symptoms of trauma with a lot of shame and impatience. And they tend to be self-critical and feel a lot of shame about how these symptoms have affected themselves and others. It will help to remind yourself from time to time that the very behaviors you feel the most shame about are actually coping methods and survival skills. They're not this powerful and persistent because you are stupid or bad—quite the contrary. They were clever and effective ways for you to cope with sometimes unbearable anxiety, fear, pain, and shame.

No matter what your past or present mistakes, no matter whether you continue to be victimized or have become abusive toward others or yourself, by practicing *self-understanding*—an important component of self-compassion—you can learn that your childhood environment likely set you up for your current behavior. By connecting compassionately with the suffering you have experienced, your self-awareness will eventually lead to self-empowerment.

8   Self-Forgiveness

True confession consists in telling our deed in such
a way that our soul is changed in the telling it.

—Maude Petre

Everything you have read in this book so far, and all the processes
and exercises you have completed, has led to this chapter. Self-
forgiveness is the most powerful step you can take to rid yourself of
debilitating shame. And absolutely nothing is as important for your
overall healing from the abuse and the effects of the abuse.

Self-forgiveness is not only recommended for those working to
heal from abuse and its effects—it's essential. It works like this: the
more shame you heal, the more you will be able to see yourself
clearly—the good and the bad. Instead of hardening your heart and
pushing people away, you will become more receptive to others and
to their feedback. You will be able to recognize and admit how you
have harmed yourself and others. Your relationships with others will
change and deepen. More importantly, your relationship with yourself will improve.

While compassion is the antidote to shame, self-forgiveness is
the healing medicine. Self-compassion acts to neutralize the poison
of shame, to remove the toxins created by shame. Self-forgiveness
acts to soothe body, mind, and soul from the pain caused by shame
and facilitates the overall healing process.

What do you need to forgive? First and foremost, you need to
forgive yourself for the abuse itself and stop making yourself its pris-
oner. As Judith Viorst, author of the wonderful book *Necessary*

Losses, writes, guilt can become a sentence to "a lifetime of penance" (1986, 136)—for a crime you didn't commit. As I've mentioned before, victims tend to blame themselves for the abuse because it's preferable to feeling vulnerable and out of control. If you continue to blame yourself for the abuse, you can continue to hold onto the illusion of control and avoid the feelings of helplessness that accompanied the abuse. And equally importantly, if you continue to blame yourself for what your abuser did, you don't have to face the feelings of abandonment, betrayal, and disappointment that go hand in hand with facing the truth about someone you cared about.

Next, you need to forgive yourself for the ways you have hurt others as a result of your abuse. This includes all your actions and omissions—all the ways you have caused others damage. Finally, you need to forgive yourself for the ways you have harmed yourself because of the abuse. In this chapter I will guide you through these three tasks.

The Obstacles to Self-Forgiveness

Just as you may have had a lot of resistance to self-compassion, you might also resist the idea of self-forgiveness. Perhaps you view self-forgiveness as letting yourself off the hook—as if self-judgment is the only way to improve. But negative self-judgment and self-blame can actually act as obstacles to self-improvement. The more shame you feel about your past actions and behaviors, the more your self-esteem is lowered and the less you will feel motivated to change. And without self-forgiveness your level of shame will cause you to defend yourself from taking on any more of it by refusing to see your faults and not being open to criticism or correction.

The good news is you can resolve to change your behavior *and* forgive yourself at the same time. In fact, the more you forgive yourself, the more you will be motivated to change. Self-forgiveness opens the door to change by releasing resistance and deepening your connection to yourself.

Another obstacle to self-forgiveness is that you may have a need to protect or forgive your abusers. But it's far more important that you forgive yourself. When you recognize you are not to blame for the abuse—that you were vulnerable, trusting, or simply had the bad luck to be in the abuser's vicinity, you may find you feel more forgiving of yourself and are freed up to feel your righteous anger toward your abuser.

Still another reason you may have difficulty forgiving yourself is that you may have a powerful need to "be good" and be seen as "all good" in the eyes of others, as well as yourself. This need to be "all good" may have started because your parents or other caretakers had this unreasonable expectation of you, perhaps severely punishing or abandoning you when you made a mistake. Now you may find you are equally critical and unforgiving of yourself.

Finally, you may ask, "Why should I forgive myself? It won't help those I've harmed." The most powerful reason: If you don't forgive yourself, the shame you carry will compel you to continue to act in harmful ways toward others and yourself. And forgiving yourself will help you to heal another layer of shame and free you to continue becoming a better human being. Without the burden of self-hatred you have been carrying around you can literally transform your life.

Forgiving Yourself for the Abuse Itself

Self-forgiveness begins and ends with the abuse itself. Hopefully, much of what you've read thus far has helped you stop blaming yourself. But for some people, no matter how many times they hear they are not to blame for the abuse they suffered as a child, they simply don't believe it. They're convinced that they are somehow responsible for the abuse occurring. This is particularly true for those who were abused by their parents and those who were sexually abused. There are reasons why these types of abuse are particularly difficult to stop blaming oneself for, as we'll discuss in this section.

Getting Past Your Denial

The main reason those who were abused by their parents or other significant caretakers tend to continue to blame themselves for the abuse is denial. As we discussed earlier, denial is a powerful defense mechanism that protects us from intense pain and trauma. It is what allows us to block out or "forget" intense pain caused by severe physical and emotional trauma. Victims of childhood abuse and neglect tend to deny what happened to them and minimize the damage it caused them, because not to do so is to face the sometimes unbearable pain of admitting that family members could treat them in such horrendous ways.

One of the main reasons for this is that children love their parents so much that they tend to idealize them. The conviction that parents are always right and that even acts of cruelty are expressions of their love is deeply rooted in each of us from the first months of life. Children are so dependent on their parents' love and care that, in order to preserve their faith in their parents, they must reject the obvious conclusion that something is terribly wrong with an abusive parent's behavior. Instead, they will go to any lengths to construct an explanation for their fate that absolves their parents of blame and responsibility. Unable to escape or alter the unbearable reality that their parent is in fact being unloving, cruel, or abusive, children alter it in their minds. The abuse is either walled off from conscious awareness and memory, so that in the child's mind it did not really happen; or it is minimized, rationalized, and excused, so that whatever did happen was "not really abuse."

The most common way children explain neglectful or abusive behavior on their parents' part is to blame themselves. Children tend to be egocentric anyway, assuming they are the cause of everything, and needing to protect their attachment to their parents only magnifies this tendency.

When we are adults, another reason for denial is that facing the truth about how our parents or other caretakers mistreated us can bring up a number of troublesome issues:

❀ What kind of a relationship with my parents (or other family members) will I be able to have once I face what they did to me?

❀ Will I need to confront my parents about their mistreatment of me in order to heal and break the cycle?

❀ Are my children safe around the people who abused or neglected me?

Some victims would rather not face the truth than have to deal with these issues. If you have any of these concerns, don't let them get in the way of your facing the truth about what happened to you. You deserve to know the truth. It really will set you free. It will help you rid yourself of your debilitating shame and break the cycle so you don't treat those you love in the same ways you were treated.

It's incredibly painful to continue to face the truth, and you will likely go in and out of denial. It takes time and courage to accept that the people you love most and who are supposed to love you are also capable of neglecting or abusing you. It takes time to comprehend that the same people who were good to you at times were also neglectful or cruel. It takes strength and time to process the pain of abuse, neglect, betrayal, abandonment, and rejection you felt as a child and still feel today. Give yourself the time you need to become strong enough to face what you have to face, to develop the support system you'll need to have in place so you won't feel so alone as you emotionally separate from your abuser(s). And you'll need to be patient with yourself when you waffle back and forth about what is true and what isn't.

Abuser Traits

Those who become abusive tend to have certain predictable traits, attitudes, and behavior patterns; learning about these patterns can help you accept that you were not to blame for the abuse. Most of these traits and behaviors result from the fact that abusers themselves were abused emotionally, physically, or sexually as children. (Please note: these traits most accurately describe those who become emotionally or physically abusive. Those who become sexually abusive may not have these same traits.) If you have been a victim of emotional or physical abuse as a child (or even as an adult), see if you recognize your abuser below.

Those who become abusive often have:

- A childhood background involving emotional, physical, or sexual abuse and/or abandonment

- A tendency to blame others for their problems

- A strong desire to remain in control, a fear of being out of control, and/or a need for power and control

- Difficulty empathizing with others (or inability to empathize)

- An inability to respect interpersonal boundaries, or even a compulsion to violate boundaries

- A tendency to be unreasonable or have unreasonable expectations of children, partners, and relationships

- Repressed anger

- An uncontrollable temper or very short fuse

- A tendency to be emotionally needy or demanding; a dependent personality

- Poor impulse control

- Intense fear of abandonment

- High levels of stress and high arousal levels

- Poor coping skills

- Selfishness and narcissism

- A history of being abusive (physically, verbally, and sexually) as an adult or older child

The fact that abusers share patterns of traits and behavior means this: *you didn't cause the abuser(s) in your life to become abusive.* You couldn't have. They were already abusive before you were born or before they met you. They didn't emotionally or physically abuse you because you were stubborn, because you didn't listen, because you talked back, because you were a difficult child. They abused you because their emotional makeup and background made it all but inevitable. These people were ticking time bombs, just waiting to go off. You just happened to be in the vicinity when they did.

Abuser Beliefs

In addition to common background and personality characteristics, those who become emotionally or physically abusive tend to have certain beliefs about themselves and others that set them up to become abusive. These beliefs set the tone for the relationship and can be abusive in themselves; they include:

- ❀ The abusers are always right.

- ❀ It's always someone else's fault.

- ❀ Their own needs are more important than others' needs.

- ❀ They have a right to expect others to do as they demand, and if someone refuses, she is the enemy.

- ❀ They are superior to or otherwise better than most people— smarter, more competent, more powerful—and therefore they *deserve* special treatment or consideration.

- ❀ It's not important what others are feeling.

- ❀ Those who complain about their behavior are too sensitive or too demanding.

- ❀ No one can be trusted, and others are constantly out to get them.

Again, if one or both of your parents (or an adult partner) has many of the above beliefs, this person has an *abusive personality*. This means that this person is abusive in most of his or her relationships, especially when he or she has all the power—as is the case when the relationship is with a child.

Knowing there is such a thing as an abusive personality—and what it looks like—can help you recognize there is only one person responsible for abusing a child: the person doing the abusing. It is never the child's fault. Stop blaming yourself for the abuse—it was not your fault, no matter what the circumstances. There is absolutely nothing a child can do to warrant abuse.

Forgiving Yourself for Being Sexually Abused

Victims of childhood sexual abuse typically feel a great deal of shame for the abuse itself, and this shame may cause them to be self-destructive: by abusing their bodies with food, alcohol, drugs, cigarettes, or self-mutilation; by being accident-prone; by sabotaging their success; or by eliciting punishment from others. Your shame may have caused you to tenaciously hold onto your problems and your pain because it gives you the punishment you feel you deserve. You may have spent your life punishing yourself with one bad relationship after another or one illness after another.

Even though you know from an intellectual, logical viewpoint that the sexual abuse wasn't your fault, deep down inside you may not have forgiven yourself for your involvement in the abuse. For example, you may blame yourself for being submissive or passive and for not fighting the person off; you may blame yourself for not telling someone about the abuse; or you may feel shame because of the way your body responded to the abuser's touch.

Remembering You Were a Child

Many victims continue to feel shame and to blame themselves because they believe they "consented" to the sexual abuse. But it's very important for you to understand once and for all that you cannot be held responsible for any so-called choices you made concerning the sexual abuse, because you could not make a *free choice*. A free choice is made when you understand the consequences of your actions and when you are not coerced, bribed, intimidated, or threatened into satisfying someone else. You were only a child and incapable of making such a decision. We now understand that even teenagers' brains are not developed fully enough for them to be able to make free, conscious choices.

Forgiving yourself for the abuse will be easier if you continue to remind yourself of the fact that you were just a child when it occurred. Victims of abuse often feel older than they actually were at the time, sometimes because they were given adult responsibilities when they were children, sometimes because their parents treated them like adults when it came to their expectations of how they should behave, sometimes because they had already experienced so much pain. But make no mistake about it, no matter how much you may have felt like an adult, you were really only a child, with a child's mind and a child's body.

More importantly, remember that you did not have the power of an adult. Because you were a child you were limited in terms of what you could do to save yourself. If you tried to run away, where would you go? If you tried to tell, who would believe you? If you tried to fight back, what chance did you have of overpowering your abuser?

Exercise: Remind Yourself How Powerless a Child Really Is

1. The next time you are around children who are the age you were when you were first abused, take a close look at them. Pick a child who is the age you were then and observe him closely.

2. Notice how small the child is compared to the adults around him.

3. Think about how easy it would be for an adult or older child to physically pin down the child or otherwise prevent him from leaving.

4. Reflect on how dependent the child is on the adults around him. For example, the child may appear to be independent, but he needs his parents or caregivers to feed him, clothe him, and drive him places.

This is what my client Ryan noticed during the exercise:

"I was watching a little boy who was about nine years old. He was acting really tough, playing with some older kids while his mother talked to another woman at the mall. He was yelling and roughhousing with them and I heard him brag about how strong he was, how he had taken karate lessons. All of a sudden, one of the bigger boys grabbed one of his arms and pinned it behind him. The younger boy struggled and tried his best to get free, but couldn't. All of a sudden he seemed very small and helpless.

"The experience of watching this kid was a wake-up call for me. When I was nine I also felt really tough—like nothing or no one could hurt me. But that was just an illusion. I wasn't that tough at all. I couldn't fight off my molester. I was too small and too weak. All this time I had been fooling myself into thinking I could have fought him off if I'd wanted to. But I didn't have a chance in hell."

Forgiving Yourself for Going Back

Even if you finally come to realize that you were an innocent child who didn't *cause* the abuse or *choose* to be abused, you may still blame yourself for other aspects of the abuse, such as the fact that you kept going back to the abuser. If this is the case, think about the circumstances at the time of the abuse. Did you go back to the abuser because you were lonely and this person paid a lot of attention to you? Did he give you candy and let you play video games? Once again, remember that you were just a child. You can't be held responsible for choices you made as a child because you simply were not old enough to think clearly, decide rationally, or always do the right thing—even in terms of taking care of yourself. For a child, getting attention might outweigh the fact that she puts herself in danger by being around the molester. And you had no way of knowing just how damaging the abuse would be to your psyche.

Forgive yourself for going back. And forgive yourself for anything else you did as a child that was a consequence of the abuse, such as lying and stealing after the abuse started, initiating sex with other children, bringing other children into the situation, or hurting your pets. You were hurt and angry and full of shame. Unable to express your anger toward the perpetrator, you may have taken your anger out on those who were weaker and smaller than yourself—since you hated yourself for being weak and helpless, you hated others who were weak as well. Use the following exercise to practice the forgiveness you need and deserve.

Exercise: Forgive Yourself for Having Been Sexually Abused

1. List everything you feel shame about or blame yourself for concerning the sexual abuse. For example:

   - *I feel shame for not saying no.*

   - *I feel shame for not telling—and he went on to abuse other kids.*

   - *I blame myself for turning the abuser on.*

   - *I feel shame because I brought other boys to my abuser's house.*

   - *I blame myself because I knew my brother was molesting my sister and I didn't protect her.*

2. For each item you listed, give at least three reasons why you now believe you did it. For example:

   - *I didn't say no because I was afraid to.*

   - *I didn't say no because I thought I had to mind him.*

   - *I didn't say no because I didn't really understand what he was doing.*

3. Now complete the following sentence for each item on your list:

   I am not responsible for _____ because _____.
   For example:

   - *I am not responsible for not saying no because I was a child and thought I had to do what an adult told me to do.*

   - *I am not responsible for not telling because I was afraid he would kill me.*

4. Now complete the following sentence for each item you have listed: I forgive myself for _____. For example:

   - *I forgive myself for not saying no.*

   - *I forgive myself for not telling.*

5. After you have completed the above sentence for each item you have listed, go back and read your list out loud, taking a deep breath after you read each item and really letting it in.

Forgiving Your Body

If you were sexually abused, your body may have responded to the touching, no matter how much your mind fought it or felt repulsed by it. Some victims have experienced orgasms even though they were being traumatized, hated the perpetrator, or were terrified. This kind of experience can make you feel like your body betrayed you, and can sometimes be very hard to forgive. A child does not know that her body can respond without her consent, or even that it can respond in such a way. You may have felt that you must have wanted the sexual act; otherwise, why would your body feel pleasure? In addition, the perpetrator may have used the fact that your body responded to manipulate you into believing you really wanted it.

As odd as it may sound, you need to forgive your body for responding. It is especially important to forgive those parts of your body that were directly involved in the sexual acts, and the parts of your body that felt any pleasure. For example, forgive your hands for touching his penis, forgive your breasts for responding to his touch, forgive your genitals for becoming stimulated. Many victims hate their genitals because the abuser touched them.

Just as you were innocent, your body was innocent as well. Stop punishing and hating your body for doing what it was made to do—react to stimuli, respond to touch, give you pleasure when touched. Stop hating it when it is a perfectly good and normal body. Your body did not betray you. It was manipulated by the abuser, just like the rest of you.

Self-healing rituals can bring you a sense of being reborn, cleaned, and refreshed. Combining them with the following writing exercise can be a powerful way of working on forgiving your body.

Exercise: Forgive and Cleanse Your Body

1. For each part of your body that was involved in the sexual abuse or that you feel betrayed you, complete the following sentence: "I forgive you, _____, for _____."

2. Soak in a hot bath or Jacuzzi. Imagine that all the residues of the abuse, especially your feelings of shame and self-blame, are being soaked *out* of you through your skin. Visualize the shame and impurities flowing out of your genitals, breasts, mouth, anus—any part of your body that was "contaminated" by the abuser.

3. Now imagine pouring compassion and loving energy *into* your body. Visualize your body being transformed into one that is wholesome, pure, and free of shame. Emerge from the water feeling cleansed inside and out.

Forgiving Yourself for the Harm You Caused Others

Forgiving yourself for the ways you have hurt or harmed others will probably be the hardest thing you will ever have to do to heal your shame. In fact, it may be the hardest thing you ever have to do in your life. This is especially true if you have repeated the cycle of abuse by harming another person in the same ways you were abused.

For example, it may seem impossible to forgive yourself for abusing a child. After all, you know firsthand how much child abuse damages a child. And you know firsthand how much the shame that accompanies abuse can devastate a person's life. Here are some examples of what clients have shared with me regarding the shame they felt:

⚘ "How could I possibly abuse my own child the way I was abused? I knew how much it devastated me to be beaten by my father. And yet I turned right around and did it to my own children. It's unforgivable."

⚘ "I promised myself I wouldn't treat my children the way I was treated. And yet to my horror the very same words my mother said to me came out of my mouth. Those horrible, shaming, devastating words: 'I hate you. I wish you had never been born.' How can I forgive myself for saying those horrible words to the people I love most in the world?"

⚘ "I feel like a monster. The shame I feel for molesting my daughter is so intense I can't even describe it. I couldn't have done anything worse to her. I've affected her life in such a horrible way. She must feel so betrayed. She must hate me and I don't blame her."

As difficult as it may seem to be able to forgive yourself for the harm you have caused others, the good news is that there are several effective ways to go about it, outlined in the pages that follow. These include: (1) deepening your self-understanding, (2) cultivating a sense of common humanity, (3) taking steps to earn your forgiveness, and (4) asking for forgiveness from a higher power.

As you read more about each of these approaches, think about which ones you relate to the most—the avenues that resonate the most with you and your situation.

Self-Understanding Can Lead to Self-Forgiveness

We spent much of the last chapter building your self-understanding around the behaviors and symptoms that are aftereffects of your abuse. If you continue to remind yourself that *it is understandable that you would have repeated the cycle of abuse given how you suffered as a child,* you will be able to take responsibility for your actions without further shaming yourself. And now that you have more understanding as to why you have acted as you have, you are more likely to be willing to forgive yourself for your negative actions and behaviors. Understanding that the trauma you experienced created problems within you that were out of your control can go a long way toward helping you forgive yourself for the ways you have hurt others. For example, understanding that your addiction—whether to alcohol, drugs, sex, food, shopping, or gambling—has been a way to self-medicate and cope with anxiety and fear can help you stop beating yourself up for the harm your addiction caused those close to you. Understanding that the reasons you have become abusive toward your children or your partner or have developed a pattern of allowing others to abuse you come directly from your abuse experiences can help you to stop chastising yourself for these behaviors.

Understanding Why You Became a Neglectful or Abusive Parent

The long-term effects of trauma (such as abuse in childhood) tend to be most obvious and prominent when people are stressed, in new situations, or in situations that remind them of the circumstances of their trauma. Unfortunately, becoming a parent creates all three of these circumstances for someone who was abused in childhood. First-time parenthood, in particular, is stressful and almost always triggers memories of our own childhood traumas. This sets the stage for child abuse.

In addition, the sad truth is that those who were abused or neglected in childhood are more likely to become abusive or neglectful of their own children than those who didn't have these experiences. In addition to the traits listed earlier in this chapter, there are other traits you may have that predisposed you to treat your children in abusive or neglectful ways. These include: an inability to have compassion toward your child; a tendency to take things too personally (causing you to overreact to your children's behavior); being overly invested in your children looking good (and you looking good as their parent) because of your lack of self-confidence; and an insistence on your children "minding" or respecting you to compensate for your shame or lack of confidence.

And there is another reason, not often discussed, that can cause a parent to become abusive: seeing your own weakness or vulnerability in your child. Those with a history of having been victimized may respond by hating or despising weakness. If you saw weakness in your child, you may have been reminded of your own vulnerability and victimization and this may have ignited your own self-hatred, causing you to lash out at your child.

Understanding the Key Skills of Good Parenting

Although there isn't a "parent" personality, there are certain personality characteristics that most good parents have in common: patience, flexibility, tolerance for intrusion, and the ability to put oneself aside for prolonged periods of time without experiencing deep resentment or anger. Unfortunately, those who suffered from child abuse and/or neglect often lack these personality traits, both because they didn't have good role models for them and because the trauma they experienced caused deficits in their personality development.

Other abilities necessary in order to be a good parent include the ability to:

⊛ Emotionally bond with your child

⊛ Handle stress in a positive way

⊛ Find appropriate outlets for your negative emotions

⊛ Get your needs met by the adults in your life instead of expecting your child to meet them

⊛ Have reasonable expectations of your child

⊛ Love your child unconditionally (even if you dislike some of his behavior)

⊛ Willingly devote a great deal of time and energy to taking care of your child's needs without taking your anger out on your child or inducing guilt in your child

⊛ Feel protective of your child

Once again, your own experiences of abuse and/or neglect may have prevented you from developing many of these abilities. For example, if your mother did not emotionally bond with you, you may have found it difficult if not impossible to bond with your own children; if your parents looked to you to meet needs that should have been met by other adults in their life, you may have repeated this pattern; and if your mother did not protect you from the abusers in your life, you may not have protected your own children from the abusers in theirs.

Forgive yourself. You didn't know any better. You didn't have the guidance you needed. You did the best you could.

Common Humanity and Gaining Compassion for Yourself

In Kristin Neff's construct of self-compassion, she names recognition of the common human experience—her term is "common humanity"—as the second fundamental element of self-compassion. She describes it as an awareness of "the fact that all human beings are fallible, that wrong choices and feelings of regret are inevitable" (2011, 62).

The truth is, every single person on this planet has harmed at least one other person in ways that have shaped that person's life. Knowing this, knowing that you are not alone in this way, can help you have compassion for yourself and forgive yourself. Feeling compassion for yourself doesn't release you from taking responsibility for your actions (which we'll discuss later in the chapter). But it can release you from the self-hatred that prevents you from forgiving yourself and free you to respond to the situation with clarity. Rather than tormenting yourself with guilt and shame, having compassion for your own suffering and for the suffering of those you have harmed can help you achieve the clarity necessary to think of ways you can help those you have harmed. (Again, we will discuss some of these ways in this chapter.)

Acknowledging the interconnected nature of our lives is another aspect of the concept of common humanity. The truth is, who we are, how we think, and how we behave is inextricably interwoven with other people and events. In other words, you didn't get where you are all by yourself. Your tendency to be a victim or to be abusive didn't just happen. You must continue to look for the causes and conditions that led you to these unhealthy behavior patterns.

When you examine your mistakes and failures with a view to really understanding yourself, it becomes clear that you did not consciously choose to make them; and even in those rare cases when you did make a conscious choice, the motivation for your actions was colored by your abuse experiences. Because of the shame you have carried, you may have closed your heart to others, becoming blind to how your actions were harming them. Outside circumstances also contributed to you forming your particular patterns; these include genetics, family experiences (including the way your parents interacted with each other and the way they interacted with you), and life circumstances such as economic status, family history, and cultural background.

As Kristin Neff wrote, "When we recognize that we are the product of countless factors, we don't need to take our 'personal failings' so personally....A deep understanding of interconnectedness allows us to have compassion for the fact that we're doing the best we can given the hand life has dealt us" (2011, 73).

Exercise: Your Sins and Omissions

1. Write a list of the people you have harmed and the ways you have harmed them.

2. One by one, go through your list and write down the various causes and conditions that led you to this action or inaction. You've already made the connection between your harmful actions and the fact that you were abused or neglected. Now think of other factors, such as a family history of violence or addiction, as well as more subtle factors like stress due to financial or marital problems.

3. Now consider why you didn't stop yourself from harming this person in spite of the precipitating factors. For example, were you so full of rage that you couldn't control yourself? Did you hate yourself so much that you didn't care how much you hurt someone else? Had you built up such a defensive wall that you couldn't have empathy or compassion for the person you harmed?

4. Once you feel you have a better understanding of the causes and conditions that led you to act as you did, see if you can apply the concept of common humanity to your actions in this situation: that is, acknowledge you were an imperfect, fallible human being and, like all humans sometimes do, you acted in ways that hurt someone else. Honor the limitations of your human imperfection. Have compassion for yourself. Forgive yourself.

Earning Your Forgiveness

If you continue to find yourself resisting the act of forgiving yourself, ask yourself this question: "Why wouldn't I want to forgive myself?" Since you are reading this book about ridding yourself of shame, why are you resisting completing one of the most important steps in this process? If your answer is "I don't deserve it," remind yourself that this is your shame talking. And if you are still feeling like you don't *deserve* forgiveness, perhaps you believe you need to *earn* it. The following are steps you can take toward earning forgiveness.

Taking Responsibility

How do you earn forgiveness? First of all, you need to admit to yourself and others the wrongs you have committed. Unless you tell the complete truth about how you have harmed others, first to yourself and then to the person or people you have hurt (if at all possible), you may not believe you deserve to be forgiven. (And incidentally, they may not be willing to forgive you.)

Dwelling on your mistakes does no one any good, including the person you harmed. When you take responsibility for your actions you may feel a surge of shame at the moment, but before long that feeling of shame will be replaced with feelings of self-respect and genuine pride.

To prepare yourself for this process, spend some time thinking seriously about how your actions or inaction have harmed the person. Completing the following sentences may help: "I harmed _____ by _____." or "I caused _____ to suffer in the following ways: _____." Write down all the ways your action or inaction harmed this person.

The next step is to go to those you have harmed and admit what you have done to hurt them. It's important that you understand that those you have harmed have a right to their anger; and that you allow and, in some cases, encourage them to voice their anger directly to you. Taking responsibility may also include admitting to others, such as family members, how you abused or neglected your victim. Make certain, however, that you do not allow anyone to verbally abuse you or to shame you in this process.

Apologizing

Your admission of what you did to harm others is doubly powerful if it is accompanied by a heartfelt, sincere apology. One of the most frequent comments I hear from those who were abused in childhood is that they wish the offender would admit what he did and apologize to them for it. Think of an incident when you felt wronged by another person. What did you want from that person in order to forgive him or her? Most people say they want an apology. But why is this the case? It isn't just the words "I'm sorry" that we need to hear. We need the wrongdoer to take responsibility for her action, and we need to know that the wrongdoer feels regret or remorse for having harmed us.

Apology can remove the cloak of shame that even the most remorseful person carries around. On the other hand, if you don't experience enough shame when you wrong someone else, apology can help remind you of the harm you caused. The act of apologizing to someone usually causes us to feel humiliated or humbled. Remembering that feeling the next time you are tempted to repeat the harmful act can discourage you from doing so.

When we are able to develop the courage to admit when we are wrong and to work past our fears and resistance to apologizing, we develop a deep sense of respect in ourselves. This self-respect can in turn affect our self-esteem, our self-confidence, and our overall outlook on life. When I apologize to you, I show you that I respect you and care about your feelings. I let you know that I did not intend to hurt you and that it is my intention to treat you fairly in the future. If you apologize for abusing or neglecting a child, even if that person is now grown, you will not only validate her experience but help her stop blaming herself for the abuse.

How to Make a Meaningful Apology

A meaningful apology is one that communicates what I call the three Rs—**regret, responsibility,** and **remedy**. It includes:

❀ A statement of **regret** for having caused the inconvenience, hurt, or damage. This includes an expression of empathy toward the other person showing that you understand how your action or inaction harmed him.

❀ An acceptance of **responsibility** for your actions. For an apology to be effective, it must be clear that you are accepting total responsibility for your actions or inaction. This means not blaming anyone else for what you did and not making excuses for your actions.

❀ A statement of your willingness to take some action to **remedy** the situation. While you can't go back and undo or redo the past, you can do everything within your power to repair the harm you caused. Therefore, a meaningful apology needs to include a statement in which you offer some kind of restitution: an offer to help the other person or a promise to take action so that you will not repeat the behavior. In the case of emotional or physical abuse, you can enter therapy or a support group to make sure you do not abuse anyone again. You can offer to pay for your victim's therapy, or you can donate your time or money to organizations that work to help victims of abuse.

For more on how to make a meaningful apology, refer to my book *The Power of Apology* (2001).

Ask Your Higher Power for Forgiveness

When we face the truth about how we have hurt others, sometimes severely, the feelings of guilt and shame can be overwhelming. Often, the only way we can find self-compassion or self-forgiveness is to reach out to something bigger than our individual selves.

Whatever your religious or spiritual beliefs, asking your higher power for comfort, compassion, and forgiveness can be a powerful step in forgiving yourself. This may be as simple as praying to God to forgive you for your sins, or it may involve a more structured gesture.

For example, the act of confession within the Catholic Church is essentially an apology to God. It has all the important components of apology—a statement of regret, an acceptance of responsibility for one's actions, a promise to not repeat the offense, and a request for forgiveness. In the Jewish tradition, it has long been the custom to seek forgiveness from family members, friends, neighbors, and colleagues during the time of the High Holy Days.

You may also wish to pray to your higher power for help in your process of self-forgiveness. Many of my clients have reported that by doing this they believe they received help in this endeavor.

If you have learned from your mistake and do not wish to repeat it, then you no longer need to feel guilt or shame about it. Forgive yourself and let it go. Criticizing and judging ourselves keeps us down, robs us of our confidence and motivation to change, and prevents us from learning from our mistakes. It encourages others to judge us and keeps us in negative situations and around negative people far longer than we should stay.

If you find you are still overwhelmed with guilt or shame about how your past behavior has affected someone, it will be important that you realize and remember this truth: the most effective method of self-forgiveness is for you to vow that you will not continue the same behavior or hurt someone in the same way again.

Forgiving Yourself for Harming Yourself

Just as important as forgiving yourself for the harm you have brought to others is forgiving yourself for the harm you have caused yourself. Sometimes this harm is obvious—it's what you have done to your body by excessive drinking, drugs, smoking, or eating; eating unhealthy foods; bingeing and purging; self-mutilation; or having unsafe or promiscuous sex. Forgive yourself for all these and similar things. You didn't love and respect your body because of the massive amounts of shame you carried. You hated your body because it was a source of pain and shame. You starved your body because you had been starved of love, nurturing, and proper care when you were a child. You attacked your body because others had attacked it and you felt this was what it deserved. You were reckless with your body because no one had cherished it when you were growing up. Forgive yourself.

Forgive yourself for the things you did that damaged your spirit, your image of yourself, and your integrity. For example, forgive yourself for overspending or stealing; for losing the family's house due to gambling debts; for prostituting yourself; for having sex with married people; for having sex with people you despised; for engaging in sex acts that felt repulsive or disgusting to you.

Often the harm you have caused yourself is more subtle than the obvious harm you did to your body or your self-image. We have touched upon some of these things throughout the book, and they include pushing people away that loved you, not believing in yourself, being too hard on yourself, and setting unreasonable expectations of yourself. You need to forgive yourself for these things too. At the time, you didn't know better. You were doing the best you could. You were doing what you had been taught to do. You pushed people away because you were afraid to trust, because you didn't believe you deserved to be loved. You didn't believe in yourself because no one had believed in you as you were growing up. You were too hard on yourself because your parents and other caregivers were too critical of you and had unreasonable expectations of you. Forgive yourself.

And there are even more subtle ways you have harmed yourself that you need to forgive yourself for. Forgive yourself for being misunderstood so often by other people, and by yourself. You were misunderstood because there were layers of shame between you and other people: layers of shame that hid you from others, preventing you from being yourself or from saying what you really meant or acting the way you really wanted to; layers of shame that made you appear a certain way when you really felt another way; layers of shame that made you say one thing when you meant another. Forgive yourself for being misunderstood. It was the last thing you wanted. You wanted people to know the real you and to accept you for who you are. You wanted your feelings and your perceptions validated. You wanted to be seen and heard. Forgive yourself for not knowing how to show people who you really are and for not knowing how to express yourself in a way that allows others to understand the real you.

Exercise: Self-Forgiveness Letter

1. Write a letter asking yourself for forgiveness for all the ways you have harmed yourself, including ways you have neglected your body and ways you have treated yourself as your parents or abusers treated you. Also include ways you have harmed yourself by being too hard on yourself and harm you caused yourself by pushing other people away or behaving in ways that were misunderstood by others.

2. Don't expect yourself to write this letter in one sitting. It may take several days or even weeks to complete it. Take your time and really consider the many ways you have harmed yourself.

3. As you write, bring up all the self-compassion you can muster. If you begin to feel self-critical, stop writing. Either do one of the other self-compassion exercises in this book or reread a portion of the book that will remind you of why you acted the way you did (for example, chapter 7, on self-understanding). Then go back to your letter with self-compassion in your heart and mind.

Forgiving yourself will do more for you in terms of healing your shame than almost anything you can do. Forgive yourself for the abuse itself. You were an innocent victim who did not deserve to be abused. Forgive yourself for the ways you reenacted the abuse. You were full of shame and, as you have learned, shame causes us to do horrendous things to ourselves and others.

9   Self-Acceptance

Healing the self means committing ourselves to a wholehearted willingness to be what and who we are—beings frail and fragile, strong and passionate, neurotic and balanced, diseased and whole, partial and complete, stingy and generous, twisted and straight, storm-tossed and quiescent, bound and free.

—Paula Gunn Allen

Gaining self-acceptance can be a natural outcome of self-understanding and self-forgiveness. Once you come to understand why you have behaved as you have and have forgiven yourself for your past actions or inactions, you are more likely to be able to begin to accept yourself as you are today. Self-acceptance isn't the same as excusing your behavior or giving yourself permission to continue negative, unhealthy, or dangerous behaviors. Instead, it is an *open-heartedness* to all your shortcomings and faults. It is essentially saying to yourself: "I recognize I am not perfect but I accept myself anyway."

Unfortunately, like many former victims of child abuse, you probably find it almost impossible to view yourself in this way. Instead, you probably tend to be extremely critical and judgmental of yourself, expecting yourself to be perfect or nearly perfect, and chastising yourself mercilessly when you make a mistake or fall short of your own unreasonable expectations. And so, while forgiving yourself for your past mistakes may have helped you rid yourself of much of your debilitating shame due to childhood abuse, if you continue to be self-critical and unforgiving of your current mistakes, you will find that you continue to accumulate shame.

While there may be many things you want to change about yourself, it's important to develop acceptance of yourself just as you are today—faults, weaknesses, shortcomings, and all. Everyone yearns for unconditional love and acceptance, but this is especially true for those who were severely criticized as they were growing up. Because abused children constantly receive the message that they are not good enough, that they are a disappointment to their parents, or that they are basically unlovable, it is crucially important that you work toward self-acceptance—that you give to yourself what you always yearned for as a child.

In this chapter I am going to help you focus on changing a life-time of self-shaming behavior through the new practice of self-acceptance. It may not be easy to change your habit of shaming yourself, but you can do it.

The information and strategies here will help you to stop having unreasonable expectations of yourself and to replace them with more reasonable ones. You will learn to step out of this negative mindset and begin treating yourself with the patience, kindness, love, forgiveness, acceptance, and open-heartedness that you deserve.

I will also encourage you to do all the following:

⊛ Work on discontinuing behaviors that induce shame, including being self-critical and/or perfectionistic and comparing yourself with others.

⊛ Recognize that we all have weaknesses, shortcomings, and character flaws—this is part of being human. This does not mean that you stop trying to become a better person, but that you come to recognize the difference between what you are able to change and what you need to accept.

⊛ Confront your beliefs that you should be good all the time, never make mistakes, never hurt anyone's feelings, never break the rules. The reason this is so important is that by adhering to these beliefs you set yourself up for continual self-shaming.

⊛ Work on accepting yourself in spite of the fact that you will likely continue to make mistakes or poor choices at times. If you are able to forgive yourself for your past mistakes, it will be ludicrous for you to continue criticizing yourself for mistakes you continue to make in spite of your best intentions.

Last but not least, I will encourage you to return to the mindfulness practice you learned in chapter 6 in order to learn to accept yourself on a moment-by-moment basis and to combine mindfulness with self-compassion as a way to stop fueling your tendency to be self-critical and to judge yourself harshly.

Your Critical Inner Voice

One of the most important steps in developing self-acceptance is to begin turning off your critical inner voice and installing a more nurturing one. Everyone has a critical inner voice, but those who were abused in childhood usually have an incredibly loud, vicious, powerful one. This is due not only to the abuse you experienced (and the shame that comes with it), but also to the fact that home environments where abuse occurs are often fraught with emotional abuse. At least one parent was likely being overly controlling, domineering, or critical, and because of this you may have received negative, critical messages every day. You either heard one parent berating the other or berating your siblings, or were yourself subject to relentless criticism or demands.

When a child is subject to constant criticism, he cannot help but take these critical messages inside himself. It is as if your critical parent's voice becomes your own inner voice; this is referred to as an *introjected parent*. This critical inner voice can become as relentless and demanding as any abusive parent.

If you were abused or neglected as a child, the chances are high that your inner critic is undermining your self-worth every single day. Its voice is so insidious, so woven into the fabric of your being, that you seldom if ever recognize its devastating effect. Some experience their inner critic consciously as a thought or a "voice" (although they do not actually hear a sound), but most of us are unaware of its constant activity. Usually we only become aware of it during stressful situations when our shame is activated. For example, when you make a mistake, you might hear an inner voice that says something like "What an idiot!" or "Can't you get anything right?" Before giving an important presentation at work or a speech in front of a class or group, you might hear "You should have prepared more, you're going to make a fool of yourself" or "Everyone is going to see how nervous you are." Or you have a desire to do something, like go back to school, but inside your head you hear "Who are you kidding, you're not smart, you'll fail all your classes" or "What gives you the right to go back to school? You have responsibilities. Stop being selfish."

How to Identify Your Inner Critic

It can sometimes be difficult to identify your inner critic. The judging, critical inner voice can seem a natural, familiar part of you, and the attacks can sound reasonable and just. But with every negative judgment, every attack, your inner critic weakens you and tears down any good feelings you have about yourself.

Your inner critic has many roles. It is the part of you that:

- Sets impossible standards of perfection

- Beats you up for the smallest mistake

- Blames you when things go wrong

- Calls you names such as "stupid," "ugly," and "weak"

- Compares you to others—especially to their achievements and abilities—and finds you wanting

- Keeps track of your failures or shortcomings but doesn't remind you of your accomplishments or strengths

❁ Exaggerates your weaknesses, telling you that you "*always* screw up a relationship," "*never* finish what you started," or "*always* say stupid things"

By paying attention to your self-judgments you will realize that they are not a natural part of you at all—they were learned, most likely from one or both of your parents. In fact, these standards can actually run counter to what you yourself want, feel, or know to be true. Unfortunately, even when you realize the voice is not yours, it is difficult to separate from it. You continue to feel watched by those around you and to fear their disapproval, indifference, or rejection. And you see your own critic in others as well as hearing it inside yourself. In fact, it's very common for victims of emotional and verbal abuse to have partners who are replicas of their parents and who give them the same negative messages.

The following exercise will help you zero in on the negative messages you received from your parents.

Exercise: Your Inner Critic/Your Parents

1. Write about what your parent(s) wanted for you and from you. How did they want you to act and why? How did they communicate this, and how did it affect you?

2. Explore the ways in which your inner critic or judge acts like your parent(s). How does the way you relate to yourself reflect how they related to you?

The Pathological Inner Critic

Psychologist Eugene Sagan coined the term *pathological critic* to describe the more vicious type of inner critic that attacks and judges us so harshly. A loud, verbose pathological inner critic is enormously poisonous to your psychological health—more so, in fact, than any trauma or deprivation you have experienced. This is because you can often heal your wounds and recover from your losses, but the critic is always with you, judging you, blaming you, finding fault with you.

Your pathological inner critic motivates you toward unreachable ideals. It keeps egging you on to reach that perfect image, never letting you rest or feel satisfied but instead leaving you feeling that you are never good enough. The sad truth is that it doesn't matter what you have accomplished in life, how much success you experience, how attractive you are, or what efforts you make to raise your self-esteem—if you have a powerful inner critic who chastises you constantly or discounts your achievements at every turn, you will find it impossible to accept yourself as you are.

Answer the following questions to get a sense of how powerful your inner critic is:

- ❀ Do you spend a lot of time evaluating your performance, appearance, abilities, or past history?

- ❀ Do you set very high standards for yourself?

- ❀ Is it difficult to live up to the standards you use to judge yourself?

- ❀ Do you give yourself little breathing room to make mistakes?

- ❀ Is your underlying sense of self often determined by your beliefs about what is right and wrong?

- ❀ Is your sense of self often determined by whether you have met your own or others' standards?

- ❀ Do you spend a great deal of time worrying that you have done something wrong?

- ❀ Are you continually plagued by critical messages inside your head that you are unable to quiet?

- ❀ Do you constantly compare yourself to others or to the success of others?

- ❀ Are you often envious of others' successes or achievements?

If you answered yes to more than two of these questions, your life and your experience of life are being dominated by your inner critic.

The good news is that there are steps you can take to quiet your overactive inner critic. In this section I will offer you several ways to begin doing this. The first step is to notice how often you play the negative messages from your inner critic in your head and what the circumstances are when the messages play. The following exercise will help you begin.

Exercise: Noticing Your Critical Messages

1. Begin by noticing how often you hear critical messages inside your head. Keep track of the frequency by keeping a diary or noting on paper when you hear from your inner critic.

2. Notice when these messages tend to come up; for example, when you attempt something new, when you have accomplished something, when someone has given you a compliment.

3. It can also be helpful to actually write down the content of the critical messages you hear. This will help you determine whose voice you are hearing (perhaps your mother, your father, or another important caretaker), since the words and the tone will likely remind you of the way one or more of these people spoke to you as you were growing up (or even today).

Talking Back to Your Inner Critic

Although it will be difficult to stop your judgmental, critical inner critic, you don't have to encourage or believe it either.

Your critical voice can be activated whenever you feel vulnerable or exposed. Once activated, a shaming spiral is set in motion, with a power of its own. Therefore it's imperative that you externalize this internal dialogue, to help you make it conscious, and take away some of its power.

One way to quiet and counter your inner critic is to talk back to it. Literally. While the strategies later in the chapter will be more useful in quieting your inner critic long-term, sometimes we need to act decisively in the moment. Just as you (hopefully) would not allow a bully to relentlessly criticize or put you down, you cannot allow your inner critic to continue to wear away at your self-esteem.

Most people are very uncomfortable with the idea of talking back to their inner critic. Since your inner critic is usually created by your parents' messages to you—and may actually sound like your parents' voice—it may feel as if you are talking back to them. If you are still intimidated by your parents, this can be a frightening prospect indeed. If the idea of talking back to your critic scares you, start slowly, doing it only when you feel particularly brave or strong.

The following words and phrases have proven to be particularly powerful in silencing an inner critic. Choose those that feel good to you, that empower you, or that make you feel angry.

- ✪ "I don't believe you!"

- ✪ "This is poison. Stop it!"

- ✪ "Get off my back!"

- ✪ "That's garbage!"

- ✪ "These are lies."

- ✪ "These are the same lies my mother told me."

Countering Your Inner Critic with Compassion

Once you become more conscious of your inner critic—what it's saying and when it tends to act up—you can also begin to utilize self-compassion to counter its messages.

Just as compassion is the antidote to shame, it is also the greatest antidote to the poison of your pathological inner critic. When you are being compassionate toward yourself, you silence your pathological inner critic.

Learning to be compassionate toward yourself will also help you connect with your sense of self-worth. When you have compassion for yourself, you understand yourself. You accept yourself the way you are. You see yourself as basically good. If you make a mistake, you forgive yourself. You have reasonable expectations of yourself. You set attainable goals.

The next time you hear your inner critic chastising you about something you did or didn't do, counter it by telling yourself something like:

⊛ "I'm doing the best I can."

⊛ "I'm only human and humans make mistakes."

⊛ "Given my circumstances, this is what I am capable of at this time."

⊛ "I'm fine just the way I am."

This is not the same as making excuses for your behavior; it's just a compassionate acknowledgment that we can all fail even when we try our hardest. You will be far more motivated to try harder the next time if you talk to yourself in a kind, understanding, compassionate way.

When we attack ourselves, we stimulate certain pathways in our brain, and when we learn to be compassionate and supportive of our efforts, we stimulate different pathways (Gilbert and Procter 2006). Sometimes we are so good at stimulating inner attacks and criticisms that our ability to stimulate inner support and warmth is underdeveloped. For this reason, you may need to generate alternatives to your self-attacking thoughts. While you may never be entirely free of an inner voice that says, "What's wrong with you?" or "You're an idiot" whenever you make a mistake, you can create and reinforce the growth of a parallel and even stronger healthy inner voice. You will discover that as your healthy inner voice grows stronger, it will respond more quickly, forcefully, and believably to the attacks of your critic.

I will go into more detail about how to create this nurturing inner voice in chapter 10 and continue helping you with this in chapter 11. For now, the following exercise will help you begin to create more nurturing internal messages.

Exercise: Creating a Nurturing Inner Voice

1. Sit in a comfortable position and close your eyes. Take a few deep breaths and maintain a soothing breathing rhythm as you do this exercise.

2. Place your right hand over your heart. Hold it there and let your attention and awareness center there.

3. As you breathe in and out, visualize your heart as a flower, slowly opening up. Feel your heart filling with light and love. Allow this love to begin healing your heart of past hurts.

4. Visualize this love expanding out from your heart and spreading inside your body. Allow your body to fill with light and love. If you notice you are distracted by thoughts, gently push the thoughts aside and go back to focusing on your heart.

5. Begin to bring up a nurturing inner voice. This is neither a harsh, critical voice nor an overly sweet, indulging voice. It is a warm, kind voice that cherishes you and accepts you for who you are. In time, this voice will become your own, but for now, it can be any voice you choose: that of someone who has been kind to you, or of a beloved character in a film. If you are religious or spiritual, it can be what you imagine the voice of God, Jesus, or the Buddha would sound like.

6. Notice what this kind, loving voice is saying. Open yourself up to these words, allowing yourself to feel their impact and warmth.

7. If you don't hear any loving words, don't get upset. Some people just have a more difficult time imagining and connecting with a kind, loving part of themselves than others. If this is true for you, here are some examples of kind and loving words you can repeat to yourself while continuing to focus on filling your heart with love and light:

- *May I accept myself just as I am.*

- *May I be gentle and understanding of myself.*

- *May I give myself the compassion I need.*

- *I am lovable just as I am.*

8. Gently repeat either the words you heard from your nurturing inner voice or the words I have provided, taking in deep breaths as you do so. Continue to send love and light to your heart. Gently stroke your arm or your hair or hold your face in your hands as you do so.

9. When you are ready, gently bring your awareness back to the room.

Repeat this exercise as many times as you can in the next several weeks. It won't happen overnight, but eventually this practice can help you replace the critical voice inside you with a more nurturing inner voice. This, in turn, will help you change the way you perceive and relate to yourself.

Set More Reasonable Expectations for Yourself

Because the abuse you experienced in childhood likely included your parents having unreasonable expectations of you and punishing you when you were not perfect, you may have taken on this same unfair and punitive attitude toward yourself. You may set unreasonable expectations and goals for yourself, expecting yourself to always do things correctly and not make mistakes. And when you do make the occasional, inevitable mistake or happen to behave inappropriately, you are likely very unforgiving, chastising yourself as harshly as your parents did, or punishing yourself by starving yourself, depriving yourself of anything good, or even inflicting self-harm.

If you don't have reasonable expectations of yourself—expectations that are neither too harsh nor too lenient—you will constantly set yourself up to feel disappointed in yourself (and activate your critical inner voice) or you will not take action to reach your true potential.

A reasonable expectation is one that is reachable given your history, your present situation, and who you are today. For example, it is *reasonable* that given your history of being abused, you may suffer from low self-esteem, a strong inner critic, and unhealthy shame. It is *unreasonable* to expect that given your history you would be able to overcome these negative effects of abuse overnight. It is *reasonable*, however, to expect that by reading this book and doing the exercises in it you may begin to be able to overcome much of the damage you suffered.

Use the following exercise to understand some of your unreasonable expectations about your behavior, and to replace them with more reasonable ones.

Exercise: It Is More Reasonable

1. Think of a current behavior that you would like to change (for example, improving your parenting skills).

2. Use this format to identify an unreasonable expectation and to create a more reasonable one:

   • *Given the fact that* _____ *it is unreasonable that I* _____ .

   • *It is more reasonable that I* _____ .

Example: "Given the fact that my parents were so critical of me, it is unreasonable that I will never be critical of my own children. It is more reasonable that I can catch myself when I am being critical, acknowledge this to myself and my children, and continue to work on not being critical."

Stop Expecting Yourself to Be All Good

You may have set unreasonable expectations of yourself by expecting yourself to always be respectful, generous, patient, kind, and forgiving—in other words, to be "all good." But no one can be good all the time. We all have times when we feel petty or small-minded, or when we are selfish or angry. If we accept this fact, we can forgive ourselves for our shortcomings, vow to do better, and move on. If we expect ourselves to never be petty or selfish or angry, we are setting ourselves up for failure when our less-than-perfect side inevitably comes bursting out of us.

We often witness this phenomenon with ministers and other deeply religious people and with those who dedicate their lives to helping others—teachers, doctors, charity workers. How often have you heard of a minister being caught having an illicit affair, or of someone who is a pillar of the community being caught embezzling money or doing drugs?

The truth is, those who put themselves out to the world as being all good are the very ones who are most vulnerable to experiencing a fall from grace. We cannot put aside our less "acceptable" traits, such as selfishness or a tendency to be mean or get angry; they simply will emerge sometimes. And those who try to be all good often do so because they carry so much shame. It's as if they hope that by doing good they will erase any bad things they have done in their lives. Does any of this feel familiar to you?

Many people with a history of child abuse are extremely moralistic, with strong opinions about what is right and wrong. They may insist on rules being followed to the letter, or they may focus a great deal on the concept of sin. It is very common for victims to be extremely religious, to believe in God as a punishing god, or to hold to very rigid values and beliefs. Why? It's because they believe that if they follow strict rules of conduct they will be able to prevent their rage at being abused, and/or their own abusive tendencies, from seeping out. These same people can be deeply conflicted and subject to even more shame when their own personal behavior does not match their beliefs.

As human beings we contain within ourselves a whole spectrum of urges and potential behaviors, but our parents, upbringing, society, and religion reinforce some and discourage others. While it is important for children to learn certain social behaviors in the process of growing up, the very act of encouraging some while discouraging others creates within us what Carl Jung called a "shadow personality." The rejected qualities don't cease to exist simply because they've been denied direct expression. Instead, they live on within us and form the secondary personality that psychologists call the shadow.

The shadow is the part of us that is created when we attempt to be perfect or to deny our darker urges. However, as Jung informed us, what is disowned does not go away. It lives on within us, out of sight, out of conscious thought—an alter ego just below the threshold of awareness. Those who feel they had to disown or repress many aspects of themselves in order to be accepted by their parents and/or society in general will have a very large personal shadow.

Accepting Our Imperfections

By acknowledging, admitting, and ultimately accepting our so-called negative qualities, we take them out of the shadow and into the light where they are far less powerful—far less likely to burst out of us unexpectedly and get us into trouble. When we acknowledge and accept our so-called negative qualities they are less likely to eat away at us and cause us to feel self-critical. And if we get past our black-and-white thinking we will understand that just because we make a mistake, it does not make us bad. This is the lesson my client Carlos needed to learn.

Carlos's Story: A Need to Be Seen as All Good

Carlos came to see me because his wife had left him and he wanted to get her back. Although he had been emotionally abusive toward her for years, she had not recognized it as such. But in the past few years he had begun to be physically abusive toward her, often in front of the kids. She finally left when he pushed their son across the room.

At first, Carlos admitted that things had "gotten out of hand." He said he wanted my help so he could learn how to handle his anger better. But as time went on, Carlos began making excuses for his abusive behavior, blaming his wife for pushing him too far, and saying that his kids had started defying him because they saw their mother doing it. If he lost his temper it was because of something she had done. If he became impatient and called her names it was because she refused to change as he felt she should to be a good wife. Over and over he would tell me, "I'm a good person. I'm not the person my wife is making me out to be." Then he would go on a diatribe about how he was an award-winning schoolteacher who was beloved by his students and how he was a pillar of the community, volunteering for many causes. He prided himself on being strict but loving.

Carlos's need to see himself as all good was getting in his way of saving his marriage and, more importantly, of healing himself from his abusiveness. Since in his mind he had to be all good, he couldn't afford to admit that there was an abusive side to him. He needed to learn that the very nature of being human is to be imperfect—that we are all a combination of good and bad qualities and we all share the capacity to do both good and bad things. The more we deny our bad qualities, the larger they become, and the less of a chance we have of changing them.

Our shadow is rooted in shame. The more deeply we feel flawed and unlovable, the more desperately we try to hide our shadow qualities. Ironically, as with Carlos, the more we try to hide them, the more we feed them. Whenever we reject a part of ourselves, we confirm our belief that we are unacceptable. Like being stuck in quicksand, our frantic efforts to get away from our badness sink us deeper into the sand.

Recognizing both our "good" and "bad" qualities—and acknowledging that all of them are what makes us who we are—can help us get out of a situation where shame overwhelms us. The following exercise is a good start.

Exercise: Your "Good" and "Bad" Qualities

1. List all your so-called bad qualities—those you feel shame about and/or wish you could change.

2. List all your so-called good qualities—those aspects of yourself that you feel proud of.

3. Compare your lists. Is your list of bad qualities longer than your list of good qualities? If so, you are likely judging yourself too harshly or putting too much emphasis on your weaknesses or faults. Or is your list of good qualities much longer? If so, you are likely denying your negative qualities because it causes you too much pain to acknowledge them.

4. Now go deeper. Write about how some of your so-called good qualities can in some circumstances be negative ones. For example, wanting to help others can be a good quality until you take it to an extreme and stop taking care of your own needs, as is the case with many codependents.

5. Write about how some of your negative qualities can in some circumstances be positive. For example, another way of describing "selfish" behavior could be "taking care of yourself."

Managing Your Shadow

Once you begin acknowledging your shadow, you can work to manage and take charge of it. This involves both understanding where your shadow came from, and learning to actually honor it through the processes known as mindful inquiry and radical acceptance. (More about these processes in a little while.)

Discover the Origins of Your Shadow

As we've discussed, all children undergo a socialization process that involves learning what is acceptable and unacceptable in their family and their culture, yet the so-called unacceptable qualities don't cease to exist in the child: they are merely repressed. For example, if your parents were deeply religious and taught you that sex outside of marriage was a sin, you may have repressed your sexual desires but also found that they come bursting out of you at unexpected times and in unwelcome ways.

In addition to teaching that certain behaviors are not acceptable, many parents teach their children to repress certain feelings, thus making these feelings part of the shadow as well. A little boy falls and hurts himself and is told, "Big boys don't cry." A little girl becomes angry with her brother and screams at him and is told, "Nice girls don't get angry." An exuberant child bursts into the house after school talking a mile a minute and is told by an irritated parent, "Don't get so excited. Calm down." Thus a child can learn that her entirely natural feelings are unacceptable and must be controlled. All too often this requires the child to disown her feelings and to put them into her shadow.

A child can also be taught that his feelings are actually dangerous. If a little boy gets beaten because he dared to disagree with his father, he will learn that expressing his feelings directly is unsafe. If a little girl is locked in her room because she felt too full to eat all her dinner, she will learn that her body can betray her.

Use the following exercise to map out some of the messages you received concerning which feelings and behaviors were unacceptable.

Exercise: The Messages You Received

1. List all the messages you received from parents or other caretakers or authority figures that encouraged you to hide or disown certain aspects of yourself.

2. List all the messages you received from parents or other caretakers that may have led to your repressing your emotions.

Think about, and perhaps write about, the ways this disowning of certain aspects of yourself and the repression of certain emotions have affected your life. For example, did you disown your anger as a child only to find that you now find it difficult to express your anger or to be assertive—even when you need to? Or do you now have a problem controlling your anger?

The Creation of My Shadow

When I was growing up, my mother often told this story. One day, as she dropped me off at the babysitter and gave me her usual admonishment—"Now you be good for Mrs. Jones today"—I turned to her and said, "I have to be good for Mrs. Jones, I have to be good for you, I have to be good for my teachers, I have to be good at church. When can I be bad?"

My mother always laughed when she told this story, since in many ways she loved my precociousness. But I doubt she truly appreciated what I was trying to tell her—that I felt too much pressure to be good.

My personal shadow was created by my mother's insistence that I "be good" at all times. Because it wasn't acceptable to ever be "bad" (which meant not bothering her, not asking for things, not being loud, not insisting on getting my way, not being selfish, not wanting attention…), I learned to present a "good girl" stance, to repress my anger, and to continually try to please my mother (and others). But I also carried around a lot of shame because I knew I wasn't as good as I was pretending to be. And I was enraged because I couldn't be my true self. When I think about how this message to be all good all the time affected my life, I realize that I continued to feel like a fraud and often didn't believe I deserved any good things that came my way. Early in my life my rage caused me to act out against rules, authority figures, and society in general by shoplifting, smoking, and drinking at an early age; but mostly I internalized my rage and took it out on myself in the form of overeating, sabotaging the good things I thought I didn't deserve, and feelings of self-hatred.

Honor Your Shadow

We not only need to own our shadow, we need to honor it and find it a place in ourselves—to welcome it home. Unless we do this, we are walking around with a part of us missing. Jung urged us to embrace our less than desirable traits, urges, and desires, and to stop seeking perfection in ourselves so as to seek *wholeness* instead. Rather than trying to rid ourselves of inherently impure parts of ourselves, we should embrace ourselves in our realness: broken, mysterious, and vibrantly alive.

The next time you do something to harm another person or yourself—that is, you're confronted with your own dark side— instead of becoming overwhelmed by shame, try to view yourself in a more nurturing and kind way. Have compassion for yourself. After all, you are suffering. Why not extend your compassion to your own suffering even when you are the one creating it?

Although you still need to take full responsibility for creating a negative situation, instead of getting bogged down in self-recrimination and shame, try to view the situation with curiosity. For example, if you did something that was completely out of character—like have an affair with a coworker—ask yourself, "Since I have such strong beliefs in fidelity in marriage, what happened to me that I became so out of control that I did something I don't believe in? What is behind my drive to break my own code?" Talking to yourself in this way, with honesty and curiosity, will undoubtedly bring answers—answers that can actually help you change your behavior.

The following exercise is based on the mindfulness practice called inquiry. Try it the next time you behave in a way that upsets you, such as yelling at one of your children or being impatient with your partner.

Exercise: Mindful Inquiry

1. Sit quietly and take a few deep breaths. Ask yourself, "What do I need right now?" or "What inside me needs most attention?" or

"What wants to be accepted?" This will help you drop below your self-judgment and connect with your emotions.

2. Notice what is going on in your body. Are the muscles in your stomach contracted? Is the rest of your body tight? If so, ask yourself what emotions you might be feeling to cause your body to be so tight. You might be feeling fear: fear of failing, of not being a good parent, of your partner being critical of you or abandoning you.

3. Notice how just paying attention to the emotion of fear can cause it to diminish and, with it, the self-judgment.

4. Now add compassion. Send a message to the emotion of fear (or pain, or anger, or shame), such as "I care about this suffering" or "I care about this feeling." Sit with your feelings like you would sit with a good friend who is struggling. Repeat the words "I care about this suffering" or "I care about this feeling" several times.

The attitude of self-acceptance exemplified in the exercise above makes it safe for the frightened and vulnerable parts of your being to let themselves be known. The practices of mindfulness combined with compassion will help you stop striving for perfection in yourself and instead, learn how to love yourself into wholeness. As Tara Brach stated in her wonderful book, *Radical Acceptance* (2003), "By cultivating an unconditional accepting presence, we are no longer battling against ourselves, keeping our wild and imperfect self in a cage of judgment and mistrust. Instead, we are discovering the freedom of becoming authentic and fully alive" (40).

The concept of radical acceptance that Brach is describing is that you are already perfect just the way you are—shortcomings and all. You don't need to continually strive to become a better version of yourself; you are already wonderful. Just as a good parent loves and accepts her child just as he is, strive to love and accept yourself just as you are.

Exercise: Radical Acceptance

1. Make a list of your flaws: aspects of yourself you are ashamed of; aspects of yourself you have been working on changing.

2. Read each flaw out loud, and then say to yourself: "May I love and accept myself just as I am." Take a deep breath each time you say this phase and really take it in.

Just as you longed to feel that you belonged and that you were acceptable when you were a child, work toward believing that every aspect of yourself belongs and is acceptable.

In this chapter I presented two major avenues to self-acceptance: (1) silencing your critical inner voice and creating a more nurturing inner voice; and (2) setting more reasonable expectations of yourself, including not expecting yourself to be all good. Both of these avenues offer you powerful and effective ways to begin your journey to self-acceptance.

Above all, realize that everyone longs to be accepted for who they are. Most of us have spent our lives seeking validation and approval from others. But the truth is, if we cannot accept ourselves, we cannot expect others to accept us. And without self-acceptance, we will live in fear of being rejected.

The opposite of acceptance is rejection. If you do not accept yourself fully, you are implicitly rejecting some part of yourself. When you deny, repress, or hide any aspect of yourself, you are rejecting yourself. If you hide certain aspects, disguising who you really are, you shrink and live a partial life. But if you own all your qualities and life experiences, you flourish and expand into wholeness.

10   Self-Kindness

> In all the greatest spiritual traditions, at their heart
> is tenderness, just to be kind inside, and then
> everything rights itself. Fear rests. Confusion rests.
>
> —Pamela Wilson

This is the chapter we have been slowly working our way toward throughout the book. Self-kindness is the heart of self-compassion. In some ways it is very sad that it took all this preparation for us to reach the place where most former victims of childhood abuse will be ready, willing, and able to begin providing themselves with self-kindness. It's unfortunate that we as victims of childhood abuse have to work so hard to begin to believe that we actually deserve self-kindness, much less kindness from others. But the good news is that because of the work you have done so far, you will not have to go the rest of your life without the ability to treat yourself with kindness. You can start today.

In this chapter you'll discover what self-kindness is, what it feels like, and what providing it for yourself looks like on a practical level. I will help you find ways to begin providing it for yourself, based on what fits with your personality. As the shame from the abuse continues to lift, you will undoubtedly be more open to providing yourself with self-kindness, but I understand that it may be more difficult for some. A lifetime of shame and a lifetime of being neglected, mistreated, and abused can make it hard for you to believe you deserve self-kindness, much less to actually begin practicing it. But even if you have a very difficult time with this concept and its practice, you will find you will be able to experience the healing that comes with self-kindness if you are willing to use the suggested strategies and complete the exercises in this chapter.

In some ways you have already begun to learn to practice self-kindness, since stopping the constant self-judgment and self-criticism you have been used to, and coming to understand and accept your weaknesses and mistakes instead of condemning them, are part of self-kindness.

Being kind to oneself can come naturally to those who believe they deserve it. Unfortunately, your shame has probably kept you from feeling kind toward yourself in much the same way that it may have been difficult to accept kindness from others. You may not have believed you deserved to be treated with the same patience, tenderness, and comfort you might naturally feel for a loved one. Hopefully, with some of your shame dissipated you will be more open to believing you deserve self-kindness. You may not know how to treat yourself with loving-kindness, but if you believe you deserve it, this chapter will help you learn how to practice it.

What Does Kindness Feel Like?

What is self-kindness, exactly? Let's start by defining kindness—not with a dictionary definition, but from a feeling perspective. When you think of someone being kind, what comes to mind? What does it look like? What behaviors do you think of? What does kindness feel like?

Exercise: Words of Kindness

1. Take a few minutes to think about what words you would use to describe kindness. Write these words down on a piece of paper or in your journal.

2. Now write about what it feels like to receive someone's kindness. How does it feel in your body?

For myself, when I think of kindness, I think of someone being *gentle, patient, caring, warm, open-hearted, giving, nonjudgmental, welcoming.* When I receive kindness, it feels like a warm blanket has been wrapped around me, or like being enveloped in someone's arms. My body feels warm and relaxed.

Those of us who were abused or neglected in childhood are usually keenly aware of kindness. Most especially, we are acutely aware of when it is missing. We long for it; we look for it in the eyes, faces, and hearts of others. And if and when we receive it, we are deeply touched by it.

When I was nine years old I had my first experience with someone being truly kind to me. There was an elderly couple who lived in the house in front of us. One of their grown daughters came to visit from Alaska. She spent only two weeks with them, but during that time she changed my life. I don't know if she was kind to everyone, but her kindness toward me touched me deeply. Unlike most people I had met, she seemed to really see me. Whenever she noticed me in the yard or coming home from school, she made a point of coming out to greet me. She took an interest in me, asking me questions about school and what I liked and didn't like. On some days she would invite me inside for cookies and milk. For the short time she was visiting she made me feel like someone truly cared about me and actually looked forward to seeing me.

On the day she left she gave me a scarf, with the word "Mexico" written on it in big glittery letters and a picture of a bullfighter with a cape. I loved it. She told me that one day, when I grew up, I could travel to lots of foreign places. I kept that scarf for years, as a reminder of this lady's kindness and of the fact that there were kind people in the world. I also remembered her message about travel, and dreaming about travel made my bleak childhood more bearable.

Who has been kind to you? Who treated you with interest and concern? Who made you feel like you mattered? Remember that person in the following exercise.

Exercise: Remembering a Kind Person

1. Remember a time when someone was kind to you, either as a child or an adult. Think about how this person treated you. Did he or she talk to you in a loving way, or physically comfort you in some way?

2. See if you can remember the look on the person's face. What did this person's face convey to you (for example, acceptance, kindness, generosity of spirit)?

3. Try to remember what this person said to you. See if you can remember the person's voice, or at least what that voice conveyed to you.

4. Remember how it felt to experience this kindness. How did it make you feel? Allow yourself to sink into this feeling, really taking it in.

5. Write about how it felt to experience this kindness, especially how it made you feel about yourself and how it felt in your body.

Defining Self-Kindness

Obviously, self-kindness involves providing for yourself patience, acceptance, caring, or whatever words you used to describe kindness. But it's so much more. Self-kindness involves generating feelings of care and comfort toward oneself. It involves being tolerant of our flaws and inadequacies instead of being self-critical. It also involves learning simple tools for giving ourselves the support we need whenever we suffer, fail, or feel inadequate.

Kristin Neff (2011) stated that self-kindness involves actively comforting ourselves, responding just as we would to a dear friend in need. It involves allowing ourselves to be emotionally moved by our own pain and suffering and then asking ourselves, "How can I care for and comfort myself in this moment?"

Unfortunately, it's often difficult to learn to treat yourself with kindness if you haven't experienced it from others. It helps to mimic how a person who was kind to you treated you.

Exercise: Being Kind to Yourself

1. Think about the kindest, most compassionate person you have known—someone who has been understanding and supportive of you; perhaps a teacher, friend, or friend's parent. If you can't think of someone in your life like this, think of a kind and compassionate public figure or even a character from a book or movie.

2. Try to single out just what made you feel so cared about: this person's words, gestures, looks, or touch.

3. Try talking to yourself in the same way, using the same words or tones. If the person physically comforted you, repeat this gesture toward yourself.

4. Take a deep breath and take in the feelings of loving-kindness.

When I think about my nice lady, the most significant thing I remember is how *welcoming* she was each time she saw me. She always smiled and made me feel she was happy to see me. I remember she spoke to me in a very *gentle* way. And she was very *attentive* to me, asking me questions about myself and really listening when I answered her. She showed by her expression, her nods, and her comments that she was really listening to me. She also *validated my feelings*—when I told her I felt something, she let me know it was understandable I would feel that way.

So when I decided to replicate my experience with her as a way of learning how to provide myself with self-kindness, I made sure I included the following factors:

⊛ Making myself feel welcomed and accepted for who I am. I began smiling to myself in the mirror, as if I were saying "hello" and welcoming myself.

⊛ Paying attention to myself and taking an interest in how I was feeling. I checked in with myself every day, asking myself how I was feeling (angry, sad, afraid, guilty or ashamed?).

Then I asked myself why I was feeling like this and if there was something I needed to do to address this feeling. (I'll teach you how to do this later in the chapter.)

⊛ Making myself feel loved and accepted. I practiced talking to myself in a nurturing, accepting way instead of the self-critical way in which I was used to speaking to myself. (More about this later in the chapter.)

⊛ Validating myself. I validated my own feelings by telling myself, "It is understandable that I feel this way."

Think about how you can replicate your nice person's behavior. How can you begin to treat yourself now the way you wish you had been treated as a child?

Creating a Self-Kindness Practice

Shortly I'll take you step by step through the process of creating a self-kindness practice. This will include learning to do the following:

⊛ Soothing yourself and having compassion for yourself when you're experiencing difficulty (self-soothing)

⊛ Talking to yourself in a nurturing, accepting way (positive self-talk)

⊛ Treating your body with love and care (self-care)

⊛ Knowing what you need and providing it for yourself (self-awareness)

⊛ Becoming your own nurturing and responsive parent

Compassionate Self-Soothing

Self-soothing is something many children learn to provide for themselves as part of their natural development. It goes like this: A child begins to cry out for her mother. A responsive mother reacts quickly to her child's cries. She picks up her baby and soothes her with a gentle voice and touch. She ascertains what her baby needs— food, a diaper change, or simply to be held and comforted. This is an empathetic response, which makes the baby feel safe and reassured. From experiences like this, the infant learns in a deep way that she can get what she needs when she needs it, and that all will be okay. This unconscious experience of knowing that she will be responded to adequately and that everything will be taken care of translates into an ability to *self-soothe*.

Now let's imagine another infant and mother. This time the mother is distracted and impatient. Her baby's helplessness and the immediacy of his needs trigger her own fears and threaten her fragile sense of self. Instead of responding calmly and confidently, she acts anxious and impatient and communicates (nonverbally) to her baby that things are not safe. Instead of experiencing the relief of a soothing response, the baby feels even more anxious. And the more distressed he becomes, the more distressed his mother becomes. Even food or a clean diaper cannot soothe him because he is too overwhelmed by the quality of his mother's response.

If this mother consistently treats her child this way or in other less-than-nurturing ways (leaving him alone for long periods of time, reacting unpredictably to him—sometimes coming into the room when he cries, others times not), he is likely to grow into an adult who is unable to soothe himself effectively. He may feel off balance and distressed whenever he is in a situation that is challenging or uncertain. From these early experiences he will likely develop the expectation that things will *not* be okay; that he cannot get his needs met, and that the world is an unsafe place. Some children are also inherently more sensitive and vulnerable to nonempathetic responses.

You may have noticed that when life presents challenges you often experience an intensity of distress that feels excessive and out of control. Or you may experience a depth of hopelessness and futility that seems overwhelmingly powerful. If so, it may be because your needs were not responded to in a soothing, nurturing way when you were an infant or toddler. It may also mean that as an infant or toddler you experienced a great deal of interpersonal chaos (such as hearing your parents fighting), parental neglect, or rage. These experiences would have created an intense anxiety inside you. This doesn't mean you will never feel comfortable and confident about getting your needs met or be able to self-soothe, however. There is work you can do to repair these deficits, develop a genuine concern for your well-being, and learn to be sensitive, sympathetic, and tolerant of your distress.

Nurturing Self-Talk

When you find yourself in a distressing situation, instead of allowing yourself to become overly fearful or to obsess anxiously over what could or could not happen, you can talk to yourself in a calm, nurturing way. You could do this silently, inside your head, or, if you are alone, out loud. To start, think of the kindest words you could tell yourself—the words you most need to hear. Here are some words of kindness used by some of my clients:

"I'm so sorry you are hurting. You don't deserve to be hurting like this."

"I know how tired and stressed you are. You've been working so hard....It won't be long now until you are finished and you can rest."

Going Inside

We began the process of helping you create a nurturing inner voice in the previous chapter, on self-acceptance. Begin by *going inside*, bringing all your attention to your inner self or your feeling center. Physically, this is usually somewhere around your solar plexus; the important thing is that you find a way to disconnect from the outside world and find a quiet place in your inner world. Once your focus is on your inner self, consciously create an intimate connection with yourself. Many people don't know how to do this. Others are afraid to do it because their inner life seems like a cold, uninviting place. You can start by simply asking yourself, "How do I feel?" as many times a day as you can think to do it. You may need to prompt yourself to go inside by leaving yourself written reminders like "Check in with yourself" or "How are you feeling?"

Self-Kindness Practice: Creating a Nurturing Inner Voice

1. Sit in a comfortable position, with your feet on the ground. Take some deep breaths as you focus on going inside.

2. Bring up a nurturing but strong inner voice, one that is deeply connected to the inherent strength, goodness, and wisdom within you (your essence). If it's difficult to find a nurturing voice, begin speaking to yourself in the voice you use when you talk to a small child or a beloved pet. Or adopt the voice of someone you know who is nurturing but strong (your therapist, a twelve-step sponsor, a loving friend).

3. Whenever you find you are criticizing yourself or being hard on yourself, consciously switch to this more nurturing voice.

Make it a practice to regularly give yourself credit for the progress you have made in building your nurturing inner voice or for the good things you have done.

Carlos Revisited: Self-Soothing as a Way to Quiet the Inner Critic

Remember Carlos from the self-forgiveness chapter? Carlos was extremely defensive about the fact that he had become abusive toward his wife and children. But as we were to discover, underneath all that defensiveness lay a tremendous amount of self-criticism. Carlos was just as hard on himself as he was on his wife and kids—in fact, he was as hard on himself as his father had been on him when he was a boy.

As a way of coping with his father's unreasonable expectations and extreme criticism, Carlos had covered over his pain with his now characteristic defensiveness: he'd learned to ignore his suffering. However, as a result of my being compassionate toward him, Carlos slowly began to recognize his own suffering—to feel the deep sadness he held in his heart. Gradually, after a lot of gentle prodding, Carlos was finally able to feel compassionate toward himself. During one of our sessions, as tears streamed down his face, he said, "I didn't know I felt so much pain as a child. I didn't even know it was still inside." This was a breakthrough for Carlos.

I suggested to Carlos that the next time his inner critic began to attack him he try to connect with the pain underneath by checking inside his body for tension and heaviness. Then I suggested he address his suffering by saying to himself, "I care about this pain; I care about my suffering."

At his next session Carlos reported he had done as I suggested. "It was really awkward at first. I mean, it sounds pretty strange to think about 'going inside my body.' But I did it. What I noticed was that when I asked myself where I was holding my pain I found that my throat and my heart felt tight. And I noticed that my chest felt heavy. Then I realized that my heart actually hurt. I suddenly felt needy and vulnerable—like a real wimp. In fact, the first time I tried it I had a huge shame attack. But gradually, the more I practiced it, the more I felt my armor melting. It was pretty amazing."

Amazing indeed. If you are accustomed to self-criticism and self-judgment, any genuine gesture of kindness and understanding to your wounded places can bring about an incredible transformation inside you. Your self-compassion opens your heart and healing can begin. As it was with Carlos, you will no longer need to defend yourself by putting up a wall.

As Carlos continued to practice self-kindness, he learned to stop running away from his suffering by deliberately bringing his attention to it. This helped him finally admit that his father had been abusive toward him—something he had refused to do earlier. Once he became aware of his own pain, and his heart became tender and open to his own suffering, he was finally able to extend compassion to his wife and children. In the past, he was so bent on avoiding further shame that he could not admit he had hurt them, much less feel compassion toward them. The final step was that when the guilt and shame he felt about having repeated his father's behavior with his wife and children gradually began to subside he was freed up to discover healing ways to make amends to them.

Self-Kindness Practice: Treating Yourself Tenderly

The next time your inner critic begins to attack you or you are overwhelmed with shame, stop what you are doing and ground yourself. When you are grounded, check inside your body to see where you are feeling pain or discomfort. Like Carlos, you might feel a tightness or heaviness in your throat, stomach, or chest (heart).

Place your hand gently over your heart or on your cheek and comfort yourself by saying, "I care about this suffering. May I be free from suffering."

Caring for Your Body

Research shows that self-kindness is not just some feel-good idea that doesn't really change things. For example, one important way that self-soothing works is by triggering the release of oxytocin—the hormone of love and bonding. It has been shown that increased levels of oxytocin strongly increase feelings of trust, calm, safety, generosity, and connectedness and also facilitate the ability to feel warmth and compassion for ourselves. This is especially true when you self-soothe by touching your body gently, since physical touch releases oxytocin, which reduces fear and anxiety and counteracts the increased blood pressure and cortisol levels associated with stress (Neff 2011, 48).

There are many ways to physically soothe yourself. Many of my clients find that softly stroking their cheek or gently stroking their arms is especially comforting. Find a way that works for you to soothe yourself through touch, using the following exercise to guide you.

Self-Kindness Practice: Soothe Your Body

1. Think of the most soothing kinds of physical touch and physical comforting you have experienced. It may be a wonderful massage you received or the touch of a lover. It may be the memory of a time when one of your parents or a caretaker comforted you by stroking your hair, scratching your back, or rubbing your feet.

2. As you remember this soothing touch, pay attention to the feelings and sensations that come up. Savor these feelings.

3. Try to replicate this comforting feeling by touching yourself in a similar way. You may resist at first, telling yourself it feels better when someone else is doing it, but continue the touch and try to take in the pleasure.

4. It can be especially soothing if you talk to yourself in a kind way as you stroke your arm, your hair, or your face, or soothe your body in another way.

Give Yourself What You Need

Another aspect of self-kindness is providing yourself what you need and want in life—not just when you are in distress, but overall. To do this you must be self-aware. Self-awareness involves learning about yourself—paying attention to yourself, including your feelings and your reactions. There are many examples of how, by not being self-aware, we put ourselves in situations or force ourselves to do things that we don't really want to do. Think about how often you put your own needs aside in order to do what you think is expected of you, or in order to please someone else.

Another way self-awareness can encourage you to practice self-kindness is by allowing you to pay attention to what makes you happy, comfortable, and at peace. It is amazing how many of my clients cannot answer this question because they don't take the time to focus on these things. And many of my clients aren't connected to their bodies, since for much of their lives they have walked around being either numb or dissociated. This is especially true of those who were sexually abused as children. Others discover that because their parents ignored their physical and emotional needs, they never learned how to honor their bodies and their needs. Make a point of paying attention to when you feel good and when you feel bad. It's as simple (and as difficult) as that. The following questionnaire will help you to focus on yourself so that you can become more self-aware.

Questionnaire: What Makes You Feel Good/Bad?

1. What do you do on a regular basis that makes you feel good physically? (examples: eat right, get lots of sleep, exercise)

2. What do you do on a regular basis that makes you feel bad physically? (examples: eat too many sweets, drink too much alcohol, smoke)

3. What do you do to nurture your body? (examples: put lotion on, do yoga, have orgasms)

4. When are you most comfortable in your body? (examples: after exercise, lying on your bed surrounded by lots of pillows, after a nice bath or shower)

5. When are you most uncomfortable in your body? (examples: when you have eaten too much, when you hold your body too tight for a long period of time, when you have to sit too close to someone else)

6. What foods make your body feel especially good?

7. What foods make your body feel uncomfortable?

8. What kind of massage do you prefer—soft and gentle or firm and deep? What kind of touch feels most loving to you when your partner touches you—soft, slow, firm, comforting?

9. Do you prefer a bath or a shower? Do you like to sit in a really hot tub or Jacuzzi or does this bother you?

10. What kinds of music do you prefer if you want to relax and feel your feelings? Do you resist music that will help you connect with your feelings because you don't want to feel sad and cry? If so, is there a type of music or sound—such as soft jazz or environmental sounds—that can help you relax without eliciting pain?

These questions are intended to help you slow down and really consider what makes you feel good. Only if you know what makes you feel good can you begin to provide it for yourself. And only then can you begin to practice self-kindness to your body and soul.

Self-Kindness Practice: Your Feel-Good Journal

Buy a journal or tablet that you can keep with you (or have easy access to), where you can jot down moments of self-awareness or moments of joy. For example, when you are feeling especially good—physically, emotionally, or spiritually—pay attention to the circumstances surrounding these good feelings. You may notice that when you are with a certain person—a friend or loved one—you feel especially open and loving. Note this in your journal. You may notice that certain things in your environment make you feel happy and joyous—such as looking at the ocean, watching a sunset, seeing some beautiful flowers, or being around animals. Write them down. You may also notice that when you act a certain way you end up feeling really good about yourself: for example, when you take the risk of being really honest with someone; when you put your criticism of someone aside and feel real compassion for that person; when you stop to give yourself credit for accomplishing something difficult. Write that down. Then periodically go back and read your Feel-Good Journal as a reminder to repeat the activities listed there.

Become Your Own Nurturing, Responsive Parent

Self-kindness also includes making sure your needs are met. Since you are a victim of some kind of childhood abuse or neglect, it is highly likely that you did not have a nurturing and responsive parent. One or both of your parents may have been reenacting their own childhood abuse by neglecting or abusing you; your parents may not have known how to meet your emotional needs, or may have been too preoccupied with making a living to attend to them. For any and all of these reasons, it will be important for you to become your own nurturing, responsive parent today.

Laurel Mellin, in her outstanding book and program entitled *The Pathway: Follow the Road to Health and Happiness* (2003), explains that in order to become your own responsive parent you need to create a balance between the two extremes of depriving yourself and indulging yourself. This middle point is called "responsiveness." As we discussed earlier in this chapter, a responsive parent is keenly aware of her child's needs. If her baby cries and it isn't readily obvious why, she makes every effort to discover what his needs are. She doesn't change his diapers if he's crying because he's hungry. Neither does she try to feed him when what he really needs is to be held. And when a responsive parent discovers and fulfills her child's real needs she doesn't need to indulge the child. She doesn't need to make up for any neglectful treatment on her part. She knows she has been responsive to her child's real needs and doesn't suffer from guilty feelings.

Just as a responsive parent is aware of her child's needs, you need to become aware of and sensitive to your own needs. Once you have identified your real needs, you have more of an ability to meet them. Unfortunately, discovering our real needs is not usually that easy, especially if you had depriving or overly permissive parents.

Connecting Feelings with Needs

One way of discovering what your needs are at any given time is to check in with your feelings. Your feelings will tell you what you need if you pay close attention. The following exercise will help you make this important connection.

Self-Kindness Practice: Feelings and Needs

1. Check in with yourself several times a day by going inside and asking yourself what you're feeling. It's sometimes easier to stick with the four basic feelings of anger, sadness, fear, and guilt or shame. So you would ask yourself, "Am I feeling angry?" If the answer is no, you would go on to, "Am I feeling sad?" and so on. You may find that your answer to "What am I feeling?" is something like "lonely" or "hungry."

2. When you find a feeling, look for the corresponding need. Ask yourself, "What do I need?" Often the answer will be "I need to feel my feeling and let it fade." Answer in the simplest way rather than confusing the issue with too many details or complexities. For example, when you feel angry, you may need to speak up for yourself. When you feel sad, you may need to cry. When you are hungry, you need food. When you feel guilty, you need to apologize.

3. You might have to try on several needs before you find the one that's true for you in any given moment. You may also have many needs attached to one feeling. For example, you may feel *lonely* and your *need* may be: to call a friend; a hug from your partner; to connect with yourself.

4. Be on the alert for answers that are not truly responsive to you. For example: "I feel sad—I need some candy;" or, "I feel angry—I need to hit him." Tap into your inherent wisdom and relax into a more logical, self-nurturing answer. Ask yourself, "Okay, what do I really need?" The best answer might be "to express myself (write,

sing)"; "to get physical (walk, stomp)"; "to develop a plan"; "to learn from it (next time I will)."

Treat Yourself Differently Than Your Parents Treated You

Those of us who were neglected or abused often look at those who are motivated to take care of themselves with wonder. "Where do they get the motivation?" we ask ourselves. "Why do they care so much about their health or the way they look?" We are poignantly aware that there is something missing in us—that something that creates the kind of motivation that would cause someone to say no to a piece of cake, to get up at 6:00 in the morning in order to get to the gym before going to work, to leave an abusive partner. The missing something is self-love.

Some survivors care for their bodies but do not care for their emotions or their souls. They can spend hours working out at the gym but not even five minutes checking in with how they feel. They can spend the weekend running, biking, or climbing and not spend a moment alone connecting to their soul. Or they can devote so much time to worrying about how they look on the outside that they lose track of who they are on the inside.

Many survivors of neglect and emotional abuse treat themselves exactly the way their parents did. They end up depriving, abandoning, controlling, shaming, or ignoring themselves in many of the same ways. You may be so used to being deprived that you continue to deprive yourself. You may be so used to being shamed that you shame yourself. But you do not have to stay trapped in repeating the depriving and indulging patterns you learned from your parents. Although it's tempting to indulge yourself in order to make up for what you did not receive as a child, this will not make up for the deprivation you experienced. The only thing that will begin to make up for what you did not receive as a child is for you to become the responsive, nurturing parent to yourself that you deserved all along.

Exercise: Treating Yourself with Kindness

1. Make a list of the ways you neglect or deprive yourself of what you need.

2. Write down every example you can think of regarding how your parents neglected to take care of your needs. Focus especially on how they deprived you of your basic needs for comfort, protection, and nurturing. For example, one client wrote: "My parents were always impatient with me, hurrying me around, yelling at me to hurry up. I always felt like I was in the way or that I was irritating them when I tried to tell them about my day at school."

3. Notice how often you treat yourself in similar ways to how your parents (or other caretakers) treated you. The client mentioned above wrote: "Much to my surprise, I realized that I am always impatient with myself. I'm always telling myself to hurry up and am always angry with myself for running late. And I always have a voice in my head that tells me to shut up whenever I feel like sharing with others."

4. Write down some ideas for how you can begin to treat yourself with more kindness in order to break these negative patterns. This is what my client wrote: "I'm going to work on being a lot more patient with myself. I don't like to be late, so I'm going to start getting ready to go places sooner so I don't have to rush and so I won't be critical of myself for running late. I'm going to risk speaking up and telling people about myself more. Actually, I'm a really interesting guy and I have an unusual job, so I'm going to trust that other people want to hear about it."

My mother neglected me in many ways, including not caring for my physical needs, such as by providing me clean clothes or teaching me proper hygiene, and not taking me to the dentist. Because of this, I spent my early twenties learning how to care for my physical body and having dental work done. She also deprived me of physical affection, and this (and my sexual abuse) set me up to become sexually promiscuous. Since this was fraught with problems, I learned many years later that getting massages was a better way to make up for this deficit, and I have made a practice of getting regular massages ever since.

Recently, I visited Bali and treated myself to a massage every day (massage is very inexpensive there). I found an extremely gentle, loving, and highly skilled masseur who touched my body with such loving-kindness that it made me cry. At the end of the week I had a revelation. Here was a complete stranger treating my body with more love, concern, respect, and tenderness than I ever treat myself. This was overwhelming to me. This man had taught me how to honor my body in a way nothing else has. The impact has been profound.

A Word of Warning

As you continue to practice self-kindness, you may experience a phenomenon in which you are inundated with intense feelings of grief or other negative emotions, or with traumatic or painful memories. Your old core beliefs about yourself from childhood ("I'm unlovable"; "I'm worthless") may also emerge from your unconscious as you make the practice of self-kindness more a part of your life.

A very compassionate therapist explained this phenomenon to me in this way: When we first start working on our issues, we are like a vessel filled with feelings of shame, pain, anger, fear, and guilt. As we begin to heal—especially as we start to provide ourselves with self-compassion and self-kindness—it's as if we're pouring this kindness and compassion into that vessel. Since the vessel is already full of shame and other negative emotions, we must make room for the new positive feelings of self-kindness and love. What happens is that our shame and other negative emotions start pouring out in order to make room for the feelings of self-kindness and love. So the more kind and compassionate you are to yourself, the more that feelings of grief for all the times you felt alone and misunderstood may come pouring out.

The way to deal with this predictable situation is to address it directly, not try to push away the bad feelings. You can say, "I've been feeling really good about myself; it makes sense that old feelings of self-doubt and self-hatred might come up." Or you can address your negative feelings as you have been practicing doing—by recognizing that you are suffering and saying any of the phrases that you have been using to address and tend to your suffering.

If feelings such as grief become intense, don't panic; just allow the feelings to come forth. Allow yourself to grieve for all the times when you were in pain and there was no one to comfort you. In other words, be gentle with yourself and comfort yourself in your pain and suffering.

It will take time and practice to make self-kindness a natural part of your life. But you can learn to listen to your needs and honor them. You can learn to stop ignoring your body's signals (for example, for rest or healthy food). And by developing the ability to self-soothe you also learn to love yourself even when you make mistakes.

The good news is that there is a self-rewarding aspect to self-kindness. Every day provides you a new opportunity to meet your suffering with kindness, and every time you do this you are deepening your belief that you deserve such kindness. The more you respond to yourself kindly when you make a mistake or when things go wrong, the more you erase the damage you experienced from years of self-criticism. The more you soothe and nurture yourself when you feel sad, afraid, angry, or guilty, the less you will tend to become overwhelmed by your less than positive emotions.

Above all, remember: you deserve to be kind to yourself; you deserve to soothe yourself when you are stressed; and you deserve to know and meet your basic needs for rest, good nutrition, and connection with others—needs every human being has.

11   Self-Encouragement

If everyone received the encouragement they need to grow,
the genius in most everyone would blossom and the world
would produce abundance beyond our wildest dreams.

—Sidney Madwed

We all have goals and dreams. This chapter is about how to encourage yourself to reach your goals and dreams using self-compassion as your motivator. Whether your goal is to stop letting people walk all over you, stop being abusive, get the courage and strength to leave an abusive relationship, stop drinking or taking drugs or end another kind of addiction, stop other self-destructive or self-defeating behavior, or simply become the best version of yourself you can be, self-encouragement can help you accomplish your goal.

Self-encouragement is also the fifth and last step in developing self-compassion. This step is not only an important one in itself, but it underscores and strengthens each of the other components of self-compassion. Without self-encouragement, you will tend to slip back into old habits of self-blaming and self-criticizing instead of using self-compassion to motivate you to continue on your healing journey.

If you were lucky, you may have met one or two people as you were growing up who encouraged you—a teacher, a coach, a grandparent—but you probably mostly had people around you who tore you down and discouraged you. Unfortunately, that criticism or discouragement may have been mild compared to what now goes on inside your own head. For that reason, in this chapter we will not only focus on self-encouragement but will continue to work on eliminating the self-critical voices in your head that continue to tell you that there is something wrong with you, that you aren't as good as everyone else, that you can't accomplish what you set out to do, and that you don't deserve good things.

How Your Shame Has Been a Disability

As much as we all have dreams, we all also have regrets—things we wish we had done, things we wish we hadn't done. One of the things I regret is never learning to surf. I love to be in and around water of any kind, especially the ocean. It feels like my second home. Some of my best memories are of being in or on the water, and I especially love to watch surfers slide on top of waves or tunnel through them.

I didn't learn to surf because I was afraid, and I have never felt that comfortable in my body. I've had problems with my weight all my life, and physical education in school was a source of deep shame for me. But even though I can't surf, I've taken to going down to the ocean almost every day to watch the surfers. I get a vicarious thrill from watching them glide across the waves.

One day recently I parked my car at my usual place—a lot overlooking the beach—ready to watch the surfers and write in my journal. Right in front of and just below me I saw a man sitting on the beach taking off his wetsuit, a surfboard by his side. I noticed right away that his legs didn't move—they seemed to be paralyzed. I marveled at how he could have maneuvered his surfboard out into the ocean and wished I had been there earlier to see how he used his board. I deeply admired this man's courage and determination.

I looked around to see if he had a wheelchair nearby and if there might not be an attendant with him. I spotted the wheelchair, perhaps twenty feet away—but no attendant in sight. The man continued to work on his wetsuit and I imagined him having to crawl to get to his wheelchair if no attendant appeared. Then a young man ran down the rocks from the parking lot and asked the man if he needed help. The surfer motioned up to the parking lot, indicating where the young man could take his surfboard. Then the young man went over to the wheelchair and pushed it toward the surfer. The surfer maneuvered himself into his chair and the young man picked up the surfboard and climbed the rocks to the parking lot.

Then ever so slowly, the surfer rolled himself in his wheelchair through the sand. He had a fairly long way to go, since the beach was wide. He just kept pushing himself through the sand, stopping periodically to rest. I didn't notice anyone stopping to help him. I looked away to watch the other surfers, and when I looked back he had made his way to the bottom of a sandy embankment. He stopped there for quite a while and I figured he must be resting from his long trek. As suddenly as the first young man had appeared, a second man approached the surfer and began to help push his chair up the hill. At first, they were having a hard time, so the man turned the chair around and began to pull it up the hill. That stopped working after awhile, so he turned the chair around and started pushing again. The surfer used his arms to help push himself, but the hill proved too steep. Then a young woman came along and all three of them managed to slowly make it up the hill. I felt so triumphant as I saw them reach the top.

This entire scene moved me deeply. I will tell you why in a few minutes. But before I do, I want to ask you: How did you feel as you read about the surfer?

- ❀ Did you feel guilty because you have two good legs but don't appreciate them?

- ❀ Did you feel guilty because you don't try harder to reach your goals?

- ❀ Were you moved by the surfer's courage and determination, such that you feel inspired to work harder to reach your goals?

- ❀ Were you impressed with the surfer's patience and perseverance, and how he seemed to trust that things would work out—that someone would come when he needed them?

The way you responded tells you a lot about yourself. If the story made you feel guilty, you are being self-critical. You used this story to provide you with further evidence of how lazy or inadequate or unappreciative you are. Or you felt guilty because you compared yourself with the surfer. Your thinking might have been something like this: "Here was someone who continued trying to reach his goal in spite of his obvious disability, yet I have given up on my goals and I don't even have a good reason."

If you didn't feel guilty but instead felt moved and inspired by the surfer, you're on the right track. Self-encouragement is all about courage and determination. And while it's great to be inspired by the courage and determination of other people who have overcome disabilities, one of the goals of this chapter is for you to become inspired by your own courage and determination.

If you felt inspired by the man's patience and perseverance and impressed that he seemed to trust that things would work out, that's another positive reaction. Most goals do take patience and perseverance, and this story is a good reminder of that. And being amazed about how he seemed to trust that things would work out is an understandable reaction, especially since things probably haven't worked out for you all the time. Having this kind of trust is indeed amazing.

Of course, we don't know the surfer's story. We don't know if he had been disabled all his life and had painstakingly learned how to surf in spite of his disability, or whether he had been a surfer who had a tragic accident. We don't know if he had a loving family who supported him emotionally and gave him the strength and determination to overcome his disability and reach his dream, or if he had triumphed in spite of a neglectful or abusive childhood, as so many reading this book have done. What we can see is that this man really wanted to surf—so much that he overcame his disability to do it.

Make no mistake: the abuse you suffered as a child and the shame you have been carrying around because of it have caused you to have a disability, just as the surfer does. This is not intended to minimize the difficulties the surfer has to endure each day of his life, but it is no exaggeration, either. Your shame blinded you to your good qualities and caused you to view the world in a distorted way as surely as if you were physically blind. Your shame prevented you from hearing the positive, kind things people who cared about you told you as surely as if you were hard of hearing. And your shame impaired you, and affected your ability to reach your full physical and emotional potential as much as any physical handicap would have.

Life Without Your Handicap

There is real hope for your being able to minimize or even eliminate the effects of the emotional handicaps you have suffered from all your life. As your shame diminishes, you have the opportunity to see what life could have been like without those handicaps. You can't go back and erase your childhood and start over—the abuse has left scars. But without the shame attached to the abuse, you can see more clearly, hear more clearly, and move your body more freely. Now nothing can hold you back but habit and perhaps the fear of your newfound freedom.

I didn't tell you the story of the surfer to make you feel guilty or ashamed because you have allowed your disability to stop you from doing the things you wanted to do. Neither is it intended to make you feel bad because you don't feel grateful that you have legs that work. Rather, the story symbolizes how difficult your struggle has been and how much you have accomplished in spite of your handicaps.

Think of all the negative messages you heard and all the negative messages you took on due to your shame. Now think of all the things you have accomplished in your life in spite of the shame you carried, in spite of the critical voices in your head, in spite of the fact that you were raised to believe you couldn't accomplish what you wanted.

Now imagine that all this shame and these negative messages are a giant hump that someone put on your back. I want you to really see and feel that hump. Feel how much more difficult it has been to navigate your life carrying around that extra weight on your back. Think of how that extra weight drained you of energy and made it difficult to do many physical tasks. Think of how awkward you have felt with that hump, how much it's gotten in the way of your doing even the easiest things. Now think about how embarrassed you have been with that hump on your back—how you have imagined that people were staring at you and making fun of you because of it. Think of how often you stayed home and isolated yourself rather than venturing out and risking people's stares. That hump is your shame, slowing you down, making your life difficult, causing you to feel awkward and different and unacceptable.

Now imagine how much better you will feel with that hump off your back. Notice how much lighter you feel, how much more free you are to move around, how much you blend in with everyone else—no need to fear that others will stare at you or judge you. I hope that, through the work you have done up to this point, you have some experience of the feeling that you are no longer weighed down with shame, or made to feel different or disgusting. You no longer have to hide or isolate yourself from others. You can go out into the sunshine with your head high.

Unfortunately, since you had this hump on your back for so long, you will sometimes forget that you no longer have it, and you'll act like it's still there. So you'll need constant reminders that it's gone. You'll need encouragement to break and finally leave behind old habits such as isolating yourself, assuming others are being critical, and telling yourself you can't do something. This is what self-encouragement is for.

How to Practice Self-Encouragement

Self-encouragement means building yourself up instead of tearing yourself down. It is like being a loving parent to yourself, a parent who sees her child's potential and wants to nurture it, and feels proud of her child when he achieves his goals instead of feeling envy or resentment because she never achieved her own. It's believing in yourself and in your ability to overcome your limitations and handicaps. It's focusing on your strengths, positive attributes, and skills instead of on your weaknesses and limitations. It involves making sure you surround yourself with people who will encourage you instead of finding fault—who aren't threatened by your successes. And it means focusing on what you have accomplished instead of what you haven't.

As you create your self-encouragement practice:

- ❀ Revise your goals to better reflect what you are capable of today

- ❀ Acknowledge where you could have ended up

- ❀ Give yourself credit for what you've accomplished

- ❀ Make an honest assessment of your positive and negative qualities

- ❀ Be clear about what you want to accomplish

- ❀ Replace self-criticism with self-correction

- ❀ Be prepared for disappointments

- ❀ Be prepared for your inner saboteur

Revise Your Goals to Better Reflect What You Are Capable of Today

As we've discussed, survivors of child abuse tend to set unreasonable expectations for themselves. But there is one area of your life where this may be especially true: your hopes and dreams for yourself. Time after time I have clients say they're extremely disappointed in themselves because they haven't achieved what they set out to do in life.

This was the situation with my client Rhonda. "I've had three failed marriages so I'm obviously not good at relationships, and now I'm too old to have children. I feel like such a failure. I have so much to give—I always wanted to give to a child what I didn't get—but now I see myself being an old woman who's all alone with no family around her."

While I felt sad for Rhonda, I also wanted her to know that she wasn't alone—that there are many people from abusive or neglectful childhoods who are in the same situation. Childhood abuse, and the shame that comes with it, affects our ability to connect with others in an intimate way. This is true for many reasons, including the difficulties we have with trusting others (or the opposite, being too trusting); our inability to choose healthy partners who are capable of loving us; our tendency to choose partners who are replicas of our abusers; and our difficulty in taking in good things—including love.

When I pointed these things out to Rhonda she was surprised. She honestly hadn't thought about how the abuse she had suffered could have had such a profound effect on her ability to create the family she so desperately wanted. In this, she was like many people with an abuse history who don't easily connect the abuse with their inability to achieve certain goals.

My client Jill was also critical of herself for not accomplishing more: "I always planned on going to college and becoming a teacher. I wanted to help other kids the way one of my teachers helped me. Her name was Mrs. Kinney and she took a special interest in me. She was the first person to notice I had any talent whatsoever. She gave me hope that I could grow up and create a different kind of life for myself than the way my parents lived. But I feel like I let myself down and let her down as well. I dropped out of junior college after only one year because I didn't study."

Jill underestimated the toll the physical and emotional abuse she had endured had on her. "I would try to study but I couldn't concentrate," she said. "My mind would wander. And when I had a test coming up I'd become so anxious I couldn't think."

As is common for survivors of childhood abuse, Jill suffered from the symptoms of PTSD, one of which is difficulty concentrating. And she also suffered from performance anxiety because her mother constantly corrected her when she was a child. In her mother's eyes Jill was always doing something wrong. These two factors, plus the fact that Jill was constantly triggered by memories of her father's rages and physical abuse, explained why she had such difficulty studying.

If you are disappointed or depressed, or feel ashamed because you haven't achieved your goals, it's important that you take the time to consider just how much your abuse experiences may have affected your abilities to perform tasks or learn new information and skills, or to trust, take in good things, or choose a healthy partner.

Exercise: Your Expectations of Yourself

1. Make a list of the expectations or goals you set for yourself in the past.

2. List all the ways you imagine the abuse you suffered made it difficult for you to reach your goals.

3. Use this information to gain more compassion for yourself and to forgive yourself for not achieving past goals.

4. Now revise your list of goals and expectations to include only those that are reasonable for you to meet given who you are today and your present circumstances.

This exercise is designed to help you stop putting yourself down for what you haven't been able to accomplish, work on understanding why you weren't able to reach your goals, and revise your goals to reflect a more accurate picture of who you are and what you are capable of today. By honestly looking at what you are capable of, you actually encourage yourself to continue trying. The difference is that now you will be trying to reach obtainable goals, thus greatly enhancing your chances for success.

While I am disappointed I never learned to surf, the lesson I got from watching the disabled surfer was not "You can do anything if you set your mind to it." Instead, I was reminded that learning to surf was never a priority for me. Sure, I can look longingly at surfers today and wish I had learned, but in reality, I had other priorities. And because of these other priorities, I have other accomplishments. My primary priority as a young adult was to graduate from college. This required that I work a full-time job and go to school at night—which made graduating a very long journey indeed. But I never gave up. I not only graduated with a BA degree (my original goal), I ended up going on to get my MA and then my license as a professional counselor. Thinking about it now, I know that had I wanted to surf as much as I wanted to graduate from college, I would have achieved that goal. I pushed myself to get on the bus every night after work and go to school so I could graduate, just as the surfer pushed himself to get himself and his board to and from the ocean.

Acknowledge Where You Could Have Ended Up

I acknowledge to my clients that it is indeed sad that dreams they had didn't come true. But I also remind them that they aren't failures. In fact, I see them as successes: instead of allowing their childhoods to destroy them, they overcame abuse, neglect, and abandonment to go on to become decent human beings.

It's important for you to know that there are about five paths that people who are abused in childhood often end up taking:

1. Alcoholism, drug abuse, or some other kind of addiction

2. Severe psychological illness, often requiring psychiatric care, including being put in a mental hospital due to attempted suicide or self-harm

3. Breaking the law, often ending up being incarcerated

4. Becoming an abuser

5. Continually becoming a victim

Instead of putting yourself down for not achieving your goals, remind yourself of where you could have ended up, considering what you endured. Think about how close you actually came, in some instances, to being put in jail or a mental hospital. Or you may have actually gone down one or more of these paths for a while and had to create a new, healthier path for yourself. If so, think about how hard you've worked to stop drinking or taking drugs or being abusive. Think about the work it has taken for you to break out of destructive behaviors such as self-mutilation or sexual promiscuity or to stop compulsions around shopping, stealing, or gambling.

Give Yourself Credit for What You Have Accomplished

You couldn't have survived the abuse you suffered without courage, strength, determination, wisdom, patience, and tolerance. Think about what you endured as a child and what you had to endure as an adult because of your abusive childhood. Think about the obstacles and hardships you've had to overcome. Recognize that someone who didn't have the strength, courage, or determination that you had might not have been able to overcome these obstacles. Think about the decisions you made and how some of these decisions saved you from ending up in jail, rehab, or a mental hospital.

When I think about where I could have ended up I can't help but feel proud of myself. There were many forks in the road for me, many times when I could have chosen to go down a darker road but instead pulled myself out of a mess and started over on a brighter path. Sometimes this was breaking away from the influence of certain people; sometimes it was actively pulling myself back from the edge of danger—such as when I realized, at age forty, that I had been having blackouts while drinking and that this was a sign I was becoming an alcoholic. I took stock and realized that I had been driving drunk for years and could have killed or seriously injured someone. I stopped drinking completely for many years because I couldn't trust myself to drink just one or two drinks. Had I not done this I am certain I would have ended up a full-blown alcoholic, like so many of my relatives.

The following exercise will help you think about and write about the obstacles and hardships you've had to overcome and how your courage, strength, determination, wisdom, patience, and tolerance have led you to where you are today.

Exercise: I Feel Proud That...

1. Make a list of the positive decisions you've made that steered you onto a healthier path.

2. Now write about the things you have done that you feel proud of. (Remember, pride is the opposite of shame.)

I answered the first part of this exercise in an earlier paragraph, but this is what I wrote for the second part:

- ❀ I feel proud that I didn't end up in jail.

- ❀ I feel proud that I stopped drinking when I needed to and didn't end up hurting someone by driving drunk or becoming an alcoholic.

- ❀ I feel proud that I knew enough to not become a mother because I knew I would have been neglectful and emotionally abusive to my children.

- ❀ I feel proud of myself for recognizing when I had become emotionally abusive in my romantic relationships and for working on myself so I didn't continue to be abusive.

- ❀ I feel proud that I didn't repeat the cycle of sexual abuse by abusing other children.

- ❀ I feel proud that I have worked so hard on healing myself and becoming a better person. Proud that I never gave up.

Make an Honest Assessment of Your Qualities

It's very important to get clear about which of your personal qualities you wish to accept and which you want to work on changing. For example, there may be things about yourself that you need to change, such as continuing to mistreat your children or your partner; and there may be other aspects of your personality, such as shyness, that you simply need to accept. The following exercise will help you gain more clarity about your various qualities.

Exercise: Your Qualities

1. List all your positive qualities, abilities, talents, and areas of growth (for example, sense of humor, intelligence, generosity, courage, ability to empathize with others). In particular, identify the strengths, attributes, and skills that helped you overcome the abuse from your childhood.

2. List all your negative qualities and traits, your limitations, and your bad habits.

3. Now read over your list of positive qualities and really take them in. Allow yourself to feel the pride that comes from acknowledging that you do, in fact, possess these good qualities.

4. Read over your list of negative or less-than-perfect qualities. Try to be neutral and nonjudgmental, simply acknowledging these aspects of yourself without becoming self-critical. For example, say to yourself, "It's true that I tend to be impatient and critical and that I lack much athletic ability."

5. Decide which of your less-than-perfect qualities you wish to work on and which ones you need to simply accept. For example, "I wish I was not so impatient and critical and I am working on it. As far as my lack of athletic ability, I think I just need to accept that I will never be very athletic."

6. Pick one or two qualities that you want to focus on changing. Make sure they are traits or behaviors that you actually have some control over—such as taking better care of your body or not being as judgmental of other people.

Be Clear About What You Want to Accomplish

Now that you have a better perspective surrounding past goals and expectations, you are in a better position to consider who you want to become in the future and what goals you want to set for yourself. It's important that you be clear on what your goals actually are—that you be as specific as you can. The preceding exercise may have helped you become clear about personality characteristics or behaviors that you wish to change. It is also important that you make sure that your goals are actually your own, coming from inside you, rather than things you think you should do or are feeling pressured to do. For example, if one of your goals is to lose weight, make sure you aren't doing this because your partner is pressuring you. The following exercise will help you refine your goal setting.

Exercise: Clarify Your Goal

1. State your goal as clearly and simply as you can, either out loud or on paper.

2. Write about why you want to accomplish this goal.

3. List at least three reasons why accomplishing this goal will make your life better. Please note, some reasons for accomplishing your goal, such as proving yourself to others or gaining control, success, or accolades, are motivated by a need to defend against shame and are therefore not healthy reasons for aspiring to something. Make sure your goals are self-compassionate ones, set in an effort to make your life better or to heal your suffering.

As you think about and write about your goal, you may notice some resistance or fear coming up. You might hear your pesky inner critic telling you that you can't accomplish this goal, or you don't deserve to accomplish it. Or you could notice that real fear comes up. Here are some examples of fears my clients reported:

❀ "I'm afraid that if I lose weight guys will starting coming on to me" (a survivor of sexual abuse).

❀ "I'm afraid if I leave my husband no other man will love me and I'll be all alone" (a survivor of emotional child abuse and a victim of domestic violence).

❀ "I'm afraid if I stop drinking I will have to leave my husband" (a survivor of emotional abuse and an alcohol abuser).

❀ "I'm afraid if I open up to people I will get hurt again" (a survivor of childhood neglect).

If fear does come up, allow yourself to acknowledge and feel it instead of trying to push it down or ignore it. We discussed the importance of "leaning in" to your feelings earlier in the book. For many people, simply admitting the fear helps to dissipate it. Leaning in to fear does not mean getting lost in your fear. In fact, leaning in can help you become aware and free in the midst of your experience. You can even talk to your fear to discover what it is trying to tell you, as in the following exercise.

Exercise: What Is Your Fear Telling You?

1. Begin by allowing yourself to feel the fear in your body. Fear is often felt as tightness in the throat or stomach, or tension or tightness in your jaw, neck, shoulders, chest, hands, or other parts of your body.

2. Now ask your fear, "What are you trying to tell me?" or "What do you need from me?"

3. Close your eyes, take a few deep breaths, and listen deeply to see if you hear fear's voice inside you or if you get a sense of what your fear is telling you.

When they did the preceding exercise, clients have reported hearing everything from "I want you to accept me" to information that helped them understand their fear better. It is also important to determine whether it is a fear based on reality or if it is based on shame. The fear of my client who was afraid that men would come on to her was based on reality: when she lost weight, men probably would come on to her. This is a common fear for survivors of sexual abuse. Knowing that the fear was real helped this client to focus on learning ways she could deal with the situation, including ways to assert and protect herself.

The client who was afraid she'd never find another man to love her was not dealing with a fear based on reality, since the truth was that she would very likely find other men who would love her and she wouldn't end up all alone. Her fear was based on shame. It was reinforced by the fact that her husband had often told her she was so ugly and stupid and crazy that no man could love her, and she had grown to believe him. I encouraged her to continue to deepen her self-compassion practice to rid herself of the shame she felt due to the abuse she had experienced from both her husband and from her parents.

Continuing to deepen your self-compassion practice will probably help you with most of your fears. Research shows that self-compassionate people are less afraid of failure (Germer and Neff 2013). As your shame continues to subside, you will find that you feel more and more like you deserve good things, including being able to reach your goals. Try saying to yourself (out loud is preferable), "I deserve to reach my goal"; or state your goal specifically, such as "I deserve to lose weight" or "I deserve to have a good relationship in which I am respected and loved." If you find you can't say these words and believe what you are saying, it is probably your shame working against you.

If your goal is to stop an addictive behavior and you are not already in a twelve-step program, I urge you to join one. Being with others who have the same problem and who share your struggles with shame will be immensely beneficial for you. It will also help you counteract the feelings of isolation that often go hand in hand with shame.

Also, deep healing is possible when we are in a group of people who share the same issues (for example, groups for survivors of sexual abuse or for codependents) and feelings. Being able to share your deepest thoughts and deepest shame in a group of people who will not judge you will help you to continue to heal and, therefore, help you achieve your goals.

Replace Self-Criticism with Self-Correction

One of the most significant steps in developing self-encouragement as a practice is to make the distinction between self-criticism and self-correction. Paying attention to this distinction will help you to give up self-criticism.

Paul Gilbert, in his book *The Compassionate Mind,* offers excellent insight into the differences between the two. First of all, self-criticism is shame-focused, while self-correction is compassion-focused. Because of this, there is a huge difference in how we feel when we receive the two. When you engage in self-criticism, you often feel disappointment, anger, and frustration with yourself, and sometimes even self-contempt.

When you are self-critical, you are usually looking backward and focusing, with regret, on what you did or didn't do, often in a self-punishing way. This doesn't encourage you to do better in the future—in fact, it often undermines your confidence. Compassionate self-correction, on the other hand, is forward-thinking. With self-correction, the focus is on the desire to improve and on learning from past mistakes.

Self-criticism can blind you to the positive emotions and desires within you and can fool you into believing that only if you have a stick at your back will you reach your goals. Self-correction focuses on growth rather than perfection, and any suggestions you give yourself for growth or change are given with encouragement, support, and kindness (Gilbert 2009).

Another way of comparing self-correction with self-criticism is to imagine that you are learning a new skill and that you have two instructors who trade off teaching you on alternating weeks. Your first instructor is a critical teacher who focuses on your mistakes, points out what you are doing wrong, and appears slightly irritated with you, as if he thinks you aren't concentrating or trying your hardest. The other teacher is a compassionate one who recognizes that learning new skills can be difficult and is generally kind and supportive. He focuses on what you do well and builds on that. When you make a mistake or have difficulty learning a particular thing, he praises your efforts and tries to develop an understanding of where the difficulty lies. He gives you clear and accurate feedback on how to improve your performance. He doesn't become irritated with you when you make mistakes or have difficulty catching on, but gives you the message that making mistakes is part of the learning process.

Which of these two teachers would you prefer to work with? Which teacher do you feel is going to help you learn a new skill or behavior better? You can probably intuitively sense you would learn much better with the compassionate approach. And yet you may still hold onto the idea that self-criticism, and that pesky inner critic, serves you in some way. You may still tend to believe that if you give up self-criticism you will become lazy and won't achieve as much. You might still believe what you were told as a child—that criticism keeps you humble and prevents you from becoming arrogant or conceited. It makes sense that it will continue to be difficult for you to give up these ideas completely. Nevertheless, I encourage you to make a commitment to switch to compassionate self-correction. Even though you won't be able to give up self-criticism completely, by doing the best you can, step by step, you can bring yourself into more balance.

Prepare for Your Inner Critic Becoming a Saboteur

Unfortunately, sometimes the closer we come to reaching our goals and the more emotional breakthroughs we have, the louder our inner critic can become. And it has a special tendency to rear its ugly head when we are trying to make changes to our lives or break old, negative patterns, or when we are in the midst of change. It is as if there is a part of us that is bent on sabotaging anything good that comes our way.

The way your saboteur manifests itself is usually related in some way to the type of happiness or change you are experiencing. For example, if you are beginning to feel more loved and accepted by others, your saboteur is likely to cause you to behave in a manner that will elicit anger or disapproval from those you are close to. Let's say that you are feeling loved by your new boyfriend. Your saboteur doesn't want you to feel loved so it might cause you to start an argument with your boyfriend or to flirt with another guy and make your boyfriend angry. Someone who is finally feeling accepted by a group of people might find himself suddenly behaving in a way that causes the group of people to disapprove of him or turn on him. Those who experience success in changing a behavior such as overeating may suddenly notice that after losing a great deal of weight they suddenly feel out of control with food once again.

To recognize your inner saboteur:

- ❀ Notice what happens when you experience joy, pleasure, love, recognition, acceptance, or success.

- ❀ In particular, notice whether you tend to overeat, drink too much, or otherwise indulge right after you experience any of these positive things—especially when your positive feelings are related to connecting with your emotions, your body, or your sensuality or sexuality.

- ❀ Notice whether you start an argument or push others away whenever you are especially feeling accepted or loved.

Talk to Your Inner Critic in a Compassionate Way

So what can you do if you notice that you have a strong negative reaction when you are in the midst of positive changes? Instead of standing up to your inner critic, as we discussed in earlier chapters, you can now utilize the compassionate self you have been developing to let your inner critic know that you no longer need to act as he demands—that your compassionate self is going to be more in control. Remind yourself that the criticism really stems from fear and sadness and voices from the past. You now feel more powerful, more mature, and wiser than your inner critic, and you can treat him with compassion without giving in to his fearfulness (Germer 2009).

Exercise: Compassion for Your Inner Critic

1. Sit in a comfortable position and take several deep breaths. As you did previously, when you did the first exercise to begin creating a nurturing inner voice, bring your attention to your inner self or your feeling center.

2. If you have been practicing talking to yourself in a nurturing way as well as practicing self-kindness, you have been creating a compassionate self. If you can, connect now with your compassionate self. Feel the power, maturity, and wisdom of your compassionate self.

3. Determine inside yourself that you have arrived at a point in your life when your compassionate self is going to be more in control.

4. Connect with your inner critic, and remind yourself that the criticism really stems from fear and sadness.

5. Now allow your compassionate self to talk to your inner critic. Talk to him in a strong yet compassionate way, saying something to let your inner critic know that your compassionate self is in charge now.

Here are some things my clients have said to their inner critic:

"I know you mean well, but I don't need you anymore. I'm strong enough now to take care of myself."

"I'm sorry that you are frightened and angry and feeling vulnerable and that you lash out because of this. But this isn't the way it needs to be anymore. I'm going to be in charge now."

This strategy can be powerfully effective, especially if you think of your inner critic as a good yet misguided parent who just wants to protect you and keep you from harm. No matter how many negative messages your actual parent gave you, he or she may have been trying to protect you (from disappointment, rejection, or failure). And sensing this, your inner critic was created in order to keep your parent with you. But now you no longer need this inner critic, this introjected parent. Now you have inside you a more compassionate self who will protect you in a more loving way, without all the negative messages and warnings.

I've had clients report noticing that, when things are going well for them, they begin driving dangerously, accidentally bang their body into the furniture, or feel suddenly compelled to spend too much money. Once they became aware of the power of their inner saboteur, many became even more determined—and able—to work toward their goal and win the battle with their inner saboteur. They continued to talk out loud to their inner saboteur and, ever so slowly, they noticed that their inner saboteur began to weaken. It still rears its head from time to time, but now they are ready. They know what to do.

In this chapter I offered you the story of the surfer, which I hope inspired you and reminded you to recognize and be proud of your accomplishments in spite of the shame that has plagued you all your life. I offered you suggestions as to how to create your own self-encouragement practice. And I encouraged you to be proud of the strength, courage, and determination that helped you to overcome one of the biggest obstacles anyone ever experiences—debilitating shame.

You will undoubtedly experience setbacks from time to time. These are the times when it will be important to pull out all your self-encouragement tools, including being kind to yourself when you are confronted with your limits and imperfections, believing in yourself and your ability to overcome your limitations, and focusing on your strengths and positive attributes instead of your weaknesses.

Remember that everyone fails sometimes—it's part of the human condition—and that every failure can be a powerful learning experience. Make a promise to yourself that if you do fall short of your goals, you will be gentle, kind, and understanding with yourself rather than critical.

Be proud of yourself for not giving up, for standing up, and for looking up. Don't let your shame rob you of what you were meant to be.

Conclusion

This is not the end but the beginning of the changes you can create in your life by practicing self-compassion. You will find that the more compassionate you are toward yourself, the more you will feel compelled to take better care of yourself and surround yourself with people who respect you and treat you well. As time goes by, you will notice that you compare yourself to other people less often; and you will find that you are able to evaluate yourself not on your performance, your looks, or the amount of money you make but by how well you are doing at taking care of your needs and providing yourself with the things you missed out on as a child. You will feel like you "fit in" more with other people, and will have less of a need to isolate yourself from others.

Most importantly, instead of continuing the cycle of violence by passing the abuse on to others, including your own children, you will begin to pass on compassion. As your ability to be self-compassionate continues to grow, you will discover that your compassion for others will grow as well. The more understanding and forgiving you are concerning your own mistakes and shortcomings, the more understanding and forgiving you will be of the mistakes and shortcomings of others. As you become less critical of yourself and stop setting such unreasonable expectations of yourself, you will become less critical of others—most especially of those closest to you, like your children or your partner. And when you stop ignoring your own pain and suffering and begin comforting and soothing yourself in times of trouble, you will find that your capacity to care for the suffering of others will increase.

While we tend to think of those whose behavior tends to fall in a victim pattern as people who have compassion for others more than themselves, this is not always the case. When a woman is being emotionally or physically abused by her partner, she may be so traumatized that she cannot recognize that her children are suffering as well. And women who were sexually abused as children are often unable to recognize the signs that their own children are being sexually abused. If they were to admit to themselves that their child was being abused, they would be confronted with memories of their own abuse. The more a woman in such a situation learns to have compassion for her own suffering, the more free she will be to see the suffering of her children.

If you are currently in an abusive relationship, know this: having compassion for your partner and what he has had to struggle with is a good thing; allowing him to continue to abuse you is not. You're not doing him any favors by allowing abusive behavior; in fact, you are adding to not only your own shame but his as well.

Once you no longer have to work as hard to defend against your shame, you will be able to take your blinders off and actually see other people's pain and suffering—including the pain and suffering you yourself may have caused. For those of you who have become abusive, this means you will be far less likely to reoffend. Once much of your shame has been eliminated, you can afford to face yourself much more honestly, including admitting when you have been abusive in the past and catching yourself when you start to become abusive in the present.

Afterword

You and I have been on an incredible journey together. I hope you have felt me with you all along the way—supporting you, encouraging you, sharing parts of my own story with you. I know it has sometimes been difficult to read the material and to do the exercises, but you found the strength, courage, and determination to keep going even when it wasn't easy. For this you should be very proud.

As shame diminishes, we begin to believe that we deserve a better life, one lived out of the shadows, where we can hold our heads up high and know we deserve to be respected, appreciated, and loved for who we are. I hope you have been able to make progress in quieting your critical inner voice and replacing it with a compassionate and nurturing voice that encourages you when things are difficult and compliments you when things are going well. And I hope you can continue to take in the good things that will inevitably come your way as you continue to heal. Most of all, I hope that instead of feeling broken and damaged, you will, more and more, feel whole and complete just the way you are.

Your self-compassion practice will hopefully become just that—a practice, something you continue for the rest of your life. If you do so, I promise you the rewards will just keep on coming.

The journey of healing from shame, both my own journey and those of my clients, has been the most rewarding of my life. It has been an honor and a privilege to go on this journey with you.

I welcome your feedback on how this book has affected you. You can email me at beverly@beverlyengel.com. You can also go to my website, http://www.beverlyengel.com, for more articles and for information on upcoming workshops and trainings.

I end by offering you a poem that was written from my heart.

To the Innocent

You were born innocent,
But that innocence was taken from you before it should have been.
You were forced to see things,
And hear things,
And feel things
That children should never experience.
Things that made you feel tainted,
And spoiled,
And damaged.
Things that robbed you of your wholeness.

You spent the rest of your life trying to wash off
The filth,
The grime,
The garbage of abuse.
You spent the rest of your life trying to return to your innocence.
Let the waters of compassion
Cleanse you of your shame.

It wasn't your fault.
It was never your fault.
You were innocent.
You were pure.
In your heart and soul you still are.

Embrace your innocence.
Let it permeate your being.
See it,
Hear it,
Feel it,
Reconnect with it,
Return to it.
It is who you really are.

References

Barnard, L. K., and J. F. Curry. 2011. "Self-Compassion: Conceptualizations, Correlates, and Interventions." *Review of General Psychology* 15: 289–303.

Brach, T. 2003. *Radical Acceptance: Embracing Your Life with the Heart of a Buddha.* New York: Bantam Dell.

Cozolino, L. 2007. *The Neuroscience of Human Relationships: Attachment and the Developing Brain.* New York: Norton.

Engel, B. 1989. *The Right to Innocence: Healing the Trauma of Childhood Sexual Abuse.* New York: Random House.

———. 2001. *The Power of Apology: Healing Steps to Transform All Your Relationships.* Hoboken, NJ: John Wiley and Sons.

———. 2002. *The Emotionally Abusive Relationship.* Hoboken, NJ: John Wiley and Sons.

———. 2005. *Honor Your Anger.* Hoboken, NJ: John Wiley and Sons.

———. 2005. *Breaking the Cycle of Abuse: How to Move Beyond Your Past to Create an Abuse-Free Future.* Hoboken, NJ: John Wiley and Sons.

———. 2008. *The Nice Girl Syndrome.* Hoboken, NJ: John Wiley and Sons.

Germer, C. 2009. *The Mindful Path to Self-Compassion: Freeing Yourself from Destructive Thoughts and Emotions.* New York: Guilford Press.

Germer, C., and K. Neff. 2013. Self-Compassion in Clinical Practice. *Journal of Clinical Psychology in Session* 69(8): 856–67.

Gilbert, P. 1997. The Evolution of Social Attractiveness and Its Role in Shame, Humiliation, Guilt, and Therapy. *British Journal of Medical Psychology* 70: 113–147.

————. 2003. Evolution, Social Roles, and Differences in Shame and Guilt. *Social Research* 70: 1205–30.

————. 2005. Compassion and Cruelty: A Biopsychosocial Approach. In *Compassion: Conceptualizations, Research, and Use in Psychotherapy*, edited by P. Gilbert. London: Routledge.

————. 2009. *The Compassionate Mind: A New Approach to Life's Challenges*. Oakland, CA: New Harbinger Publications.

Gilbert, P., and J. N. V. Miles. 2000. Sensitivity to Putdowns: Its Relationship to Perceptions of Shame, Social Anxiety, Depression, Anger and Self-Other Blame. *Personality and Individual Differences* 29: 757–74.

Gilbert, P., and S. Procter. 2006. Compassionate Mind Training for People with High Shame and Self-Criticism: Overview and Pilot Study of a Group Therapy Approach. *Clinical Psychology and Psychotherapy* 13: 353–79.

Gilligan, J. 2003. Shame, Guilt, and Violence. *Social Research* 70: 1149–80.

Harlow, C. W. 1999. Prior Abuse Reported by Inmates and Probationers. NCJ-172879. Washington, DC: U.S. Department of Justice.

Herman, Judith, M.D. 1997. *Trauma and Recovery*. New York. Basic Books.

Hirigoyen, M. F. 2000. *Stalking the Soul: Emotional Abuse and the Erosion of Identity*. New York: Helen Marx Books.

Jonsson, A., and K. Segesten. 2004. "Guilt, Shame, and Need for a Container: A Study of Post-Traumatic Stress Among Ambulance Personnel." *Accident* and *Emergency Nursing* 12: 215–23.

Kaufman, G. 1992. *Shame: The Power of Caring.* Rochester, VT: Schenkman Books.

Leary, M. R., E. B. Tate, C. E. Adams, A. B. Allen, and J. Hancock. 2007. "Self-Compassion and Reactions to Unpleasant Self-Relevant Events: The Implications of Treating Oneself Kindly." *Journal of Personality and Social Psychology* 92: 887–904.

Longe, O., F. A. Maratos, P. Gilbert, G. Evans, F. Volker, H. Rockliff, and G. Rippon. 2010. "Having a Word with Yourself: Neural Correlates of Self-Criticism and Self-Reassurance." *Neuroimage* 49: 1849–56.

MacBeth, A., and A. Gumley. 2012. "Exploring Compassion: A Meta-Analysis of the Association Between Self-Compassion and Psychopathology." *Clinical Psychology Review* 32: 545–52.

Mellin, L. 2003. *The Pathway: Follow the Road to Health and Happiness.* New York: Regan Books.

Miller, A. 1984. *For Your Own Good: Hidden Cruelty in Child-Rearing and the Roots of Violence.* New York: Farrar, Straus & Giroux.

Neff, K. D. 2003a. "The Development and Validation of a Scale to Measure Self-Compassion." *Self and Identity* 2: 223–50.

———. 2003b. "Self-Compassion: An Alternative Conceptualization of a Healthy Attitude Toward Oneself." *Self and Identity* 2: 85–101.

———. 2011. *Self-Compassion: Stop Beating Yourself Up and Leave Insecurity Behind.* New York: William Morrow.

———. 2012. "The Science of Self-Compassion." In *Wisdom and Compassion in Psychotherapy,* edited by C. K. Germer and R. Siegel. New York: Guilford Press.

Neff, K. D., K. L. Kirkpatrick, and S. S. Rude. 2007. "Self-Compassion and Adaptive Psychological Functioning." *Journal of Research in Personality* 41: 139–154.

Neff, K. D., and P. McGehee. 2010. "Self-Compassion and Psychological Resilience Among Adolescents and Young Adults." *Self and Identity* 9: 225–40.

Swan, N. 1998. "Exploring the Role of Child Abuse on Later Drug Abuse." *NIDA Notes* 13.

Tangney, J. P., and R. L. Dearing. 2002. *Shame and Guilt.* New York: Guilford Press.

Thompson, B. L., and J. Waltz. 2008. "Self-Compassion and PTSD Symptom Severity." *Journal of Traumatic Stress* 21: 556–58.

U.S. Department of Health and Human Services. 2013. "Long-Term Consequences of Child Abuse and Neglect." Washington, DC: Child Welfare Information Gateway.

Vettese, L. C., C. E. Dyer, W. L. Li, and C. Wekerle. 2011. "Does Self-Compassion Mitigate the Association Between Childhood Maltreatment and Later Emotional Regulation Difficulties?" *International Journal of Mental Health and Addiction* 9: 480–91.

Viorst, J. 1986. *Necessary Losses: The Loves, Illusions, Dependencies, and Impossible Expectations That All of Us Have to Give Up in Order to Grow.* New York: Free Press.

Beverly Engel, LMFT, is a licensed marriage and family therapist with over thirty years of experience working primarily with survivors of childhood and adult abuse. She is considered one of the world's leading experts on emotional abuse recovery and is author of twenty nonfiction books on the subjects of emotional and sexual abuse recovery, relationship issues, and female empowerment. Her books include *The Emotionally Abused Woman, The Emotionally Abusive Relationship,* and *Healing Your Emotional Self.* She has appeared on many national television shows, including *Oprah* and *Starting Over,* has appeared on CNN, and was nominated for the Books for a Better Life Award for her powerful book, *The Power of Apology.*

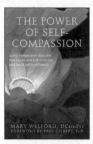
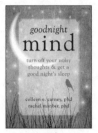

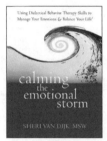

ARE YOU SEEKING A CBT THERAPIST?

The Association for Behavioral & Cognitive Therapies (ABCT) Find-a-Therapist service offers a list of therapists schooled in CBT techniques. Therapists listed are licensed professionals who have met the membership requirements of ABCT and who have chosen to appear in the directory.

Please visit www.abct.org and click on *Find a Therapist*.